Twice the First
Quirino Cristiani and the Animated Feature Film

T0136254

The Focus Animation Series aims to provide unique, accessible content that may not otherwise be published. We allow researchers, academics, and professionals the ability to quickly publish high-impact, current literature in the field of animation for a global audience. This series is a fine complement to the existing, robust animation titles available through CRC Press/Focal Press.

Series Editor Giannalberto Bendazzi, currently an independent scholar, is a former Visiting Professor of History of Animation at the Nanyang Technological University in Singapore and a former professor at the Università degli Studi di Milano. We welcome any submissions to help grow the wonderful content we are striving to provide to the animation community: **giannalbertobendazzi@gmail.com.**

Published:

Giannalberto Bendazzi; *Twice the First: Quirino Cristiani and the Animated Feature Film*

Forthcoming:

Pamela Taylor Turner; *Infinite Animation: The Life and Work of Adam Beckett*

Lina X. Aguirre; *Experimental Animation in Contemporary Latin America*

Cinzia Bottini; *Redesigning Animation: United Productions of America*

Maria Roberta Novielli; *Floating Worlds: A Short History of Japanese Animation*

Marco Bellano; *Václav Trojan: Music Composition in Czech Animated Films*

Twice the First
Quirino Cristiani and the Animated Feature Film

Giannalberto Bendazzi

Foreword by
John Halas

CRC Press
Taylor & Francis Group
Boca Raton London New York

CRC Press is an imprint of the
Taylor & Francis Group, an **informa** business
A FOCAL PRESS BOOK

CRC Press
Taylor & Francis Group
6000 Broken Sound Parkway NW, Suite 300
Boca Raton, FL 33487-2742

© 2018 by Taylor & Francis Group, LLC
CRC Press is an imprint of Taylor & Francis Group, an Informa business

No claim to original U.S. Government works

Printed on acid-free paper

International Standard Book Number-13: 978-1-1385-5446-7 (Hardback)

Library of Congress Cataloging-in-Publication Data

Names: Bendazzi, Giannalberto, author.
Title: Twice the first : Quirino Cristiani and the animated feature film / Giannalberto Bendazzi.
Other titles: Due volte l'oceano. English
Description: Boca Raton : Taylor & Francis, CRC Press, 2018. | Translation of: Due volte l'oceano. | Includes bibliographical references and index.
Identifiers: LCCN 2017027474 | ISBN 9781138554467 (hardback : alk. paper)
Subjects: LCSH: Cristiani, Quirino, 1896-1984. | Cinematographers--Argentina--Biography. | Animators--Argentina--Biography. | Animated films--History and criticism.
Classification: LCC TR849.C75 B4513 2018 | DDC 777.092 [B] --dc23
LC record available at https://lccn.loc.gov/2017027474

Visit the Taylor & Francis Web site at
http://www.taylorandfrancis.com

and the CRC Press Web site at
http://www.crcpress.com

Contents

Foreword

This book was first published in Italian in 1983 by La Casa Usher (Florence), and bore a Foreword by John Halas that we reprint here as a document.

John Halas (1912–1995) was one of the most committed advocates of animation ever. A prolific producer and director based in London, he also wrote or edited several books on the subject. In 1983 he was serving as president of ASIFA, the International Association of Animation Filmmakers.

As the production of animation gets more and more involved, influenced by the new electronic techniques and new market outlets, it is good to look back to its modest beginnings, and to discover some of the unknown aspects of its past.

This book, researched and written by Giannalberto Bendazzi, is an exciting account of some facts never before revealed in the history and development of animated film, and goes a long way toward remedying the neglect that befell one of the significant pioneers of this genre, Quirino Cristiani. Among the fascinating information the reader can learn from this book, is that not all the action in cinematography took place in North America and Western Europe, but there was a transplant of European culture throughout Italy, which germinated in Argentina, and flowered in spite of what must have been a hostile and unpromising ground.

Sheer survival in such an atmosphere could only have been achieved through a firm belief in the future value of stop motion cinematography, by an enthusiastic and unselfish attitude toward this labor-intensive medium, and by excellent individual draftsmanship from Cristiani and his associates, among them Federico Valle, another Italian-born pioneer who worked with him at that time.

There is no doubt that other pioneers of that period, such as Emile Cohl in France, Winsor McCay in the United States, and later Max & Dave Fleischer in the United States, had a profound influence on Cristiani's work, but nobody would deny his incredible achievement in many uncharted fields to become the first film cartoonist to produce a full-length animated cinema film way back in 1917, some 20 years ahead of Disney's *Snow White*. How such a brave enterprise was achieved with the highly political and satirical content of the film in an atmosphere of hostile opposition from the resident establishment is still a puzzling factor. A further achievement was that, according to the evidence, both Quirino Cristiani and Federico Valle gave careful consideration to the audience's reaction to their work, an attitude that few animators would adopt, even today. Yet a further achievement was their technical experimentation with three-dimensional multiplane effects through cardboard cut-out figures. Again they were decades ahead of anyone in this technique.

The super-human industry, the perseverance with unknown technical factors in frame by frame animation, with what must have been inadequate and primitive equipment, make both Quirino Cristiani and Federico Valle historical figures deserving a place among the other giants. This book provides an important service in documenting this period, and filling in the gaps in the history of the development of animation. We are all indebted to Giannalberto Bendazzi for uncovering and revealing these past achievements. See Figures F.1 through F.4 for Quirino Cristiani as an illustrator and comic artist.

John Halas

FIGURE F.1   A page of the magazine *La Vida Moderna* No. 271, June 19, 1912, where two illustrations of the 16-year-old Quirino were accepted. (Courtesy of the Museo de la caricatura Severo Vaccaro.)

FIGURE F.2 A page of the magazine *Media Noche* No. 3, July 29, 1926. (Courtesy of Claudio Rodríguez.)

FIGURE F.3 A full-page vignette of *Media Noche* No. 1, July 15, 1926. (Courtesy of Claudio Rodríguez.)

FIGURE F.4   A page of *Humorismo Mundial* No. 1, September 7, 1926, containing the adventures of Coquita la bataclana ("the loose dancer"). (Courtesy of Claudio Rodríguez.)

About the Author

Giannalberto Bendazzi is a scholar whose book *Animation: A World History* (three tomes, 1546 pages) was published by CRC Press in 2016. He has written and edited many books on animation and on live-action cinema, and was a professor of history of animation at the University of Milan, Italy, the Nanyang Technological University, Singapore, and the Griffith University, Brisbane, Australia. His "discovery" of Quirino Cristiani and his actual meeting with him date back to 1981.

CHAPTER 1

Who and When

Having removed him from oblivion and driven him out from the other side of the planet in 1981, having personally met him, having received documents and collected his memoirs, this writer was called the "discoverer" of Quirino Cristiani.

But this "discovery" was not due to hard digging into film archives, luck or serendipity, or rhabdomantic magic; it was only due to the adoption of a standpoint.

Argentinean film historians *did* know that *El Apóstol* and *Peludópolis* had existed. What they did not take into consideration was that *animation* existed—that is, animation as an authentic branch of the film art and industry worthy of their attention. Once somebody took this as a starting point, something that might have merely been mentioned in a footnote suddenly became a significant part of the history: the birth of the animated feature film genre (1917) and the first animated feature film with a soundtrack (1931).

Who in the world is Quirino Cristiani? He is not mentioned in the more well-known books on the history of the film industry, and he was not given much space in the otherwise reputable *Historia del cine argentino* by Domingo di Núbila. Not even in the historical accounts of the animated film industry had he been talked about.

But he was, nevertheless, a great pioneer of his craft.

He directed *El Apóstol*, the first animation feature length movie in the history of the film industry (1917), in an era in which features themselves were still experimental, in a country where the movie industry was still in the embryonic stages, and at a time when animation was rare and exotic. The first Latin American films for instructional or scientific purposes were made by Cristiani, as were the first animated advertisements on that continent. He was the only person who regularly produced short films of this type during the 1920s and 1930s. He also holds another prestigious record: he made the first animated feature film with sound that the world had ever seen (*Peludópolis*, 1931). And finally, he deserves the credit for having trained other animators in his studio, who later made important contributions toward further developments in this branch of the movie industry.

It comes naturally to ask why such an important person had been virtually ignored.

There are probably several reasons.

The first is certainly related to Quirino Cristiani's personality. He had a tendency to express himself with playfulness and irony, and was able to see himself in an ironic light. A man like this should never handle his own promotional campaigns.

The second reason is connected to the nature of animated films. Only in recent years have scholars dedicated their attention to this genre, which seems easy to understand and is unique in several different ways. Animated films were not considered of interest for many years (with the exception of Disney's films, of course) and were only mentioned in extreme cases. In choosing this branch of moviemaking, Cristiani secluded himself in an obscure and ignored sector.

The third reason can be attributed to the way historians record the history of the film industry. This discipline was developed by European researchers who were not Spanish, or by Americans who did not understand the Spanish language. Thus,

Hispanic and Latin American film makers were neglected as a category, and to complicate things, they were also badly distributed and geographically distant. Argentinean cinema falls into this category.

Finally, we need to remember that Argentinean journalists and critics, who probably wrote an occasional article about Cristiani, rarely realized how important his work was and never decided to study him in depth.

From an aesthetic standpoint, no one will ever be able to determine the value of Quirino Cristiani's films. Unfortunately, almost all of them are lost forever, and only if someone stumbles onto some forgotten footage will scholars and film buffs be able to partially satisfy their curiosity in the future. In 1926, a fire destroyed the warehouses of the producer Federico Valle, and all the copies of *El Apóstol* that were inside went up in smoke. In 1957 and 1961, two other fires devastated Quirino Cristiani's own warehouses, and turned all of his production from the 1920s up to the time to ashes. The feature film *Sin dejar rastro*, finished in 1918, was confiscated for political reasons after just one day in the theater, and from that moment on, has never been seen again.

A solid critical opinion of his works can only be given based on the one film that still remains: the short sound film *El mono relojero* from 1938 (the copy survived because it was owned by editor and producer Constancio C. Vigil, who had commissioned the work from Cristiani). That film demonstrated ordinary technical and artistic abilities, and a considerable influence from American cartoons. It is an average film, similar to many others produced at that time.

However, *El mono relojero* is probably the least suitable work to give us an authentic idea of the style and quality of Cristiani's films because it is easy to detect the conflict between the director's playfulness and the more serious tendencies of the writer Constancio C. Vigil. In addition, it was made with a different technique than the one Cristiani had invented and perfected for more than 20 years (using cut-out figures). Finally, this short film was made for children and based on imaginative elements instead of being made for adults and based on the news and politics of the day, as Cristiani preferred.

In the specific area of Argentinean cinema, Quirino Cristiani should be identified as an intellectual director (!) even though he certainly never had any intellectual ambitions. Most films produced at that time were melodramatic, such as romantic novels, and made use of tear-jerker plots, with scenes of tango dances and sentimentalism. Cristiani's films, instead, were vignettes made for an educated public who were informed about politics, and were based on references to current news and criticism of the government. These productions were above average in terms of quality.

I began working on Quirino Cristiani in 1978. Three years later, during collaboration with the provincial administration of Pavia and the municipality of Santa Giuletta, his birthplace, I was able to promote an initiative to bring Cristiani back home for a celebration, and to interview him in person. He was 85 at the time. Later, I had the chance to present my findings, which proved to be a missing chapter of film history that had not yet been written.

The current report is the best that could be done considering the difficulties. Like similar projects in other fields, the research is still in progress, and *El Apóstol* is listed among the Ten Most Wanted films by the film archives of the world.

A lengthy debate took place among the cognoscenti on the theme: Was *El Apóstol* really a feature film, or was it a … longer short? Here is this writer's opinion.

Printed documents witness that the film was screened for seven months, seven times a day; but we cannot deduce the running time from that, as we do not know the opening/closing timetable of the theatre. On the other hand, various films that have always been considered features are short according to the new millennium standards. Typical examples are Walt Disney's *Dumbo* (1941), which lasts 64 minutes, or the Russian classic *Konek goburnek* (*The Humpbacked Little Horse*, directed by Ivan Ivanov-Vano, 1947), which lasts even less than an hour: 57 minutes. He who wants to

FIGURE 1.1   President Hipólito Yrigoyen as portrayed by Valdivia.

get free from the running time idea grasp, could take into consideration that *El Apóstol* was the sole subject of the daily projections, and that the definition of feature film is "the main film on a cinema programme" (*Longman Webster English College Dictionary*, 1984). In the early days, cinema was a rather different thing from what we now consider "cinema," therefore our current categories may not correspond to the actual situation (Figure 1.1).

Foreigners know very little about the true historical and political evolution of Argentina (which is strange when we consider the importance of this country). Therefore, I thought it was a good idea to include a few appendices in this volume. The longest one contains a general timeline of the political events that happened from the end of the 1800s to the 1930s, with a particular look at President Yrigoyen and the path of radicalism. These events were the background and premise of Cristiani's films and his work as a political commentator. I have also included material to explain and describe the film industry, publishing and mass media during Cristiani's time, which will allow us to look closely at a few curious aspects of the man and his *entourage*.

REFERENCES

Cristiani, Q. (1917). *El Apóstol.*
Cristiani, Q. (1918). *Sin dejar rastro.*
Cristiani, Q. (1931). *Peludópolis.*
Cristiani, Q. (1938). *El mono relojero.*
di Núbila, D. (1960). *Historia del cine argentino.*
Ivanov-Vano, I. (1947). *The Humpbacked Little Horse.*
Longman Webster English College Dictionary. (1984). Essex, England: Longman House.
Sharpsteen, B., W. Jackson, N. Ferguson, S. Armstrong, J. Kinney, B. Roberts, and J. Elliotte. (1941). *Dumbo.*

CHAPTER 2

From Santa Giuletta to Buenos Aires

Q UIRINO CRISTIANI WAS BORN on July 2, 1896, in the village of Santa Giuletta, in Italy, which is located in the province of Pavia (Figure 2.1). His parents were Luigi Cristiani, secretary of the city administration, and Adele Martinotti.

The future director's first home was an apartment in the city hall, where the city provided lodging for its secretary and his family. Over a century has passed, and the building has been renovated and is still in use today (Figure 2.2).

Santa Giuletta is a small town originally built in medieval times on the lowest hills of the Apennines in the region known as "Oltrepo" (it means "The other side of the Po River"). It stands on a road that runs from Alessandria to Piacenza through the cities of Tortona, Voghera, Casteggio, Broni, and Stradella. At the end of the nineteenth century, its population was around 2000, just about the same as it is today. The livelihoods of citizens were, and

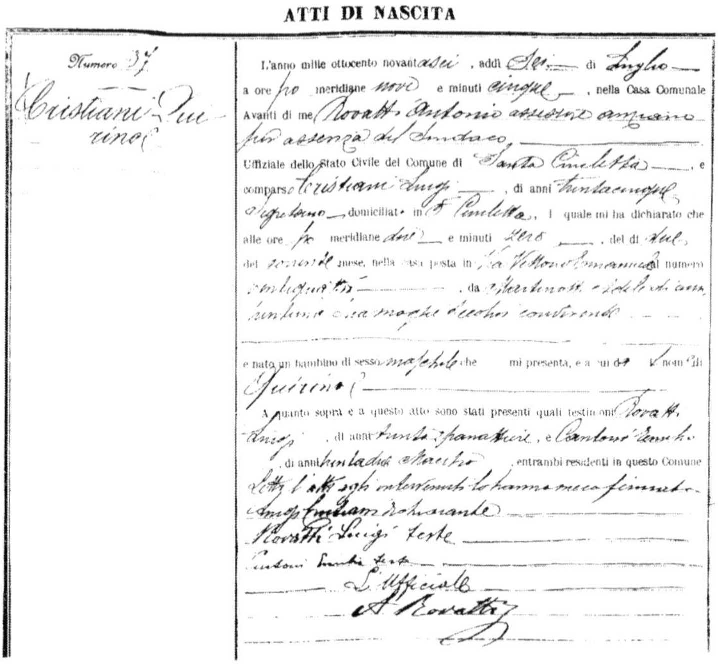

ATTI DI NASCITA

FIGURE 2.1 Quirino Cristiani's birth certificate, preserved in the municipal archives in Santa Giuletta (Italy).

still are, based on agriculture and handcrafted goods (today Santa Giuletta's prized products are wine and toys).

Quirino's parents were both from Casteggio, a small village founded in pre-Roman times about five kilometers east of Santa Giuletta at the crossroads between the road to Alessandria and Piacenza and a road that comes from Pavia. According to public records, Luigi and Adele were married there on July 24, 1884. He was 23 and worked as an elementary school teacher, and she was 19 and worked as a seamstress.

Their first child was baptized Francesco Edoardo Giulio, born in Santa Giuletta on April 4, 1885. The city records still listed the father as a teacher with residence in Casteggio. Sometime later,

FIGURE 2.2   Left, the municipal building in Santa Giuletta, Cristiani's first home, in a picture taken at the beginning of the twentieth century.

Luigi Cristiani was hired as the secretary of the city administration of Santa Giuletta. The couple had four more children after Francesco: Maria, Ines, Angela, and Quirino, of course. After the birth of their youngest, something happened to create tension between the secretary and the city council, though the nature of the problem is unknown. We do not know whether Luigi was reprimanded, nor what reasons he might have found to be at odds with the administration. However, the Cristiani family moved into a house near the Romanic church of St. Michael in Pavia, near the Ticino River. Luigi Cristiani continued to do his job, and went to Santa Giuletta every day, whereas his wife worked from home making hats to earn extra money. Between November 1899 and January 1900, the city administration decided to fire its secretary, who fought against them until they came to a compromise on February 5, 1900. According to the records, Luigi Cristiani "received the economic compensation that was due on him, and agreed to give up pursuit of any other demands."

Evidently, the Cristiani family had been talking for some time about going to the Americas. Luigi used his savings and the severance pay from his job to buy a ticket on an ocean liner and sailed to Buenos Aires.

"He was a man with a lot of dreams in his head," said Quirino of his father, "and he wanted his family to have a better life. He had been told that in Argentina they needed people who were willing to work hard, and that it was easier to make money there than in Italy."*

The other members of the family who were left in Pavia did not have to wait long to receive news. Luigi's contacts proved to be promising. With his first letter, he sent tickets for all of the others. And so, on April 11, 1900, Quirino Cristiani began his American adventure. The ship, *Messapia*, sailed from Genoa, and the poorest emigrants aboard slept in crowded, miserable conditions.†

Quirino was 4 years old. On board, he worried about the long voyage, and repeatedly asked his mother what they were going to do when they got there.

"We're going to build America," had been her answer.

This idea caused the boy's imagination to soar. In Italy, his playmates had said that there were Indians with feathers on their heads in America. When he got there, he saw that the inhabitants were just like Italians, and so he concluded that either the

---

* Throughout the rest of this book, whenever there are quotation marks with no specific reference to a speaker, it is understood that the quotation is attributed to verbal or written statements made by Quirino Cristiani to the author.

† The first official data on Italian immigration are from 1876. Between that year and 1900, a total of 4,974,000 people left the country, most from the north (3,354,000). In 1900, the year the Cristiani family left, there were 352,782 emigrants. Of those, 76,277 went to South America, and over half of those to Argentina (40,393). Lombardy contributed to the exodus with 21,401 people.

Indians had all run away or they had lost their feathers, just like white people grow bald with age.*

Luigi Cristiani had two options for work, linked to two letters of presentation. The first was addressed to Bodega Domingo Tomba, who was in San Rafael in the province of Mendoza. San Rafael was the capital of the wine industry and was located in the foothills of the Cordillera range in the Andes. It could have been a nice place to settle for people who had come from a similar area—the Oltrepo region in Italy was located in the foothills and was also famous for its wines. But Mendoza was also famous for another reason: Earthquakes. Just a short time after his arrival, Luigi Cristiani was awakened one night by an earthquake that flipped him out of bed onto the floor. He quickly went back to Buenos Aires, where he had left the family to wait for him while he assessed the situation, and decided to use the second letter of presentation. This letter recommended him for a position as an administrator of the Italian hospital. He got the job, and bought a house right in front of the hospital, in calle Gascón y Cangallo (today, Juan Domingo Perón), in the *barrio* of Almagro. The family lived there for several years, and Quirino spent his wedding night there in 1917.

---

* In 1900, Argentina was growing quickly. For centuries it had been a deserted, uninhabited place, even after winning its independence from Spain in 1810. The drive to colonize the interior started around 1860, when the population of colonists of Spanish descent numbered less than one million in a territory of three million square kilometers. The population had doubled in 1869, and in 1895, it had grown to more than four million. In 1914, there were more than eight million people, thanks to immigration. Liberal politicians had planned for this in response to their motto, *gobernar es poblar*. Italian, Spanish, Slavic, German, Syrian, and Lebanese immigrants came in droves to Buenos Aires, causing it to grow rapidly from 187,346 citizens in 1869 to 433,375 in 1887. The population continued to grow: 663,854 in 1895; 950,891 in 1904; 1,231,698 in 1909; 1,576,597 in 1914; and the latest census, in 2001, showed a population of 2,776,138.

Cristiani wrote, "When I got to Argentina, I had never seen a big city, and I was astonished. Buenos Aires was already a metropolis. They were finishing the famous Avenida de Mayo, which would later become the busiest, most crowded street in the city to compete with Calle Corrientes, which has the most stores."

CHAPTER 3

The First Years in Argentina

T HE *BARRIO* OF ALMAGRO was not a rich neighborhood. The Cristiani family managed to maintain a satisfying lifestyle, thanks to Luigi's salary and Adele's wise household management.

"My childhood and adolescence were very happy," remembered Quirino Cristiani. His father had a dream for him: he wanted Quirino to become a doctor and to work in that same Italian hospital where he worked. But the boy was passionate about drawing: he scribbled on every scrap of paper and literally left his mark on every wall in the house.

> My father used to say that artists were people who died of hunger. Since I didn't want to go to university, it was necessary that I at least learn a trade. Almost as punishment, he put me in a cobbler's shop to work as an assistant. "Do you prefer this or medicine?" he asked. I said that I would be happy to stay there, and he just laughed.

After a bit, he got me a job with an insurance company. I was just a kid, and I'm sure I was a bad employee ... But I had to earn a living! In the evenings, though, I took classes at the Academy of Fine Arts.

The future director's personality was already pretty solid: a clearly independent spirit ("soy un gran bohemia," I am a confirmed bohemian, is a recurring expression in the letters he sent to this writer), originality which resulted in small inventions, and an instinct for self-teaching. In addition, he was also a nonconformist, which permitted him not to be ashamed of his dreams (that were not profitable financially), and also to decide to become a vegetarian early on—in a country where the national dish is *asado.** Another side of his unconventional personality emerged later on in his life: he became a nudist, and founded the first Argentinean nudist colony. Creating a bit of a scandal, needless to say.

When he was 16, Quirino Cristiani entered a fine arts school. His parents thought that it was the best way for him to get some use out of his talent, or at least perfect his artistic skills. But he only lasted there for four months. He could not tolerate the hours of still life sketching. He needed something that moved, something more expressive. Furthermore, as he told this writer later on, "mi sentir no compatía con la enseñanza académica."†

And so he continued to study by himself, mainly by going to the zoo on Sundays. "I would take notes and sketch the animals in movement. I spent a lot of time watching the monkeys and chimps; who knows whether it helped me when years later I made *El mono relojero.*" At the Academy, he did have one stroke of

---

* *Asado* is grilled beef. Cristiani had good reasons for eating the way he did. He had violent headaches every time his mother convinced him to eat animal protein. When he kept refusing, she resorted to "hiding" meat in things like ravioli. Finally, she gave up. From the first decade of the twentieth century to the end of his lifetime, Quirino Cristiani never ate another bite of meat.
† Translated: "my nature is incompatible with academic education."

luck: he became friends with men and women who later became great Argentinean painters.

Pio Collivadino, Atilio Malinverno, Emilio Pettorutti, Antonio Alice, Emilia Bertolé, Lino Enea Spilimbergo, and so on. All Italians, by the grace of God and strength of the nation! Almost all great "scapigliati," *bohemios* like me; especially Spilimbergo, my lifelong friend ...*

In terms of quality, circulation, and number of publications, the Argentinean press was already considered one of the most important in the Spanish speaking world. Two large daily newspapers, *La Nación* and *La Prensa*, split the readership. Founded by liberal intellectuals and landowners, who were open to collaborating with the best minds in the country, these newspapers were considered very prestigious and formed public opinion. *La Prensa*, in particular, was a sort of Spanish-language London *Times*.

The other papers were less pretentious, and had no problems with using drawings, vignettes, and caricatures—particularly political caricatures, a specialty that Argentineans had mastered at the time of their revolutionary war. Most of these newspapers targeted the general public, but there was one among them that stood out for its intelligence and vivacity: the intellectual magazine *Caras y Caretas* (Faces and Masks).

It was printed in a small format, with lively content and plentiful foreign pieces. *Caras y Caretas* was founded in 1898 by Bartolomé Mitre (son of the ex-President of the Republic with the same name), caricaturist Manuel Mayol and Eustaquio Pellicer. It defined itself as a "semanario festivo, literario, artístico y de actualidades" and was the first Argentinean newspaper to start printing comic strips in 1912: Manuel Redondo published the adventures of Viruta and Chicharrón (*Viruta y Chicharrón* bore

---

* Spilimbergo (1896–1964) is considered to be one of Argentina's most important painters and muralists.

no signature, but is attributed to Redondo or to Juan Sanuy and others) and the story of the immigrant *Sarrasqueta* (drawn by Alonso at the outset). It is also important to remember that, right from its beginning, *Caras y Caretas* could depend on the collaboration of Diógenes "El Mono" Taborda, a caricaturist who will be presented later in this book.

> Artists had dignity in this branch of journalism, which was ready to do something about the political and social situation at the time. It would not have been easy for a young man to earn a living by just drawing vignettes, but it was certainly a good start. Hence, when Quirino Cristiani was still under 18 years of age, he decided that the environment—with its coffee, newsroom atmosphere, long discussions, and intellectual curiosity—was the place for him. First, he published his caricatures in the magazine *Sucesos,* and the director, Orts, thought well of him because he was enthusiastic and bold. Then he went to work for Evar Méndez, director of a more important publication, *La gaceta de Buenos Aires.* Cristiani's drawings were fairly successful, and a man named Federico Valle really liked them, too. In fact, Valle wasted no time in asking Cristiani to come to his office.

REFERENCE

Cristiani, Q. (1938). *El mono relojero.*

CHAPTER 4

A Meeting with Federico Valle and an Introduction to Animated Caricatures

QUIRINO CRISTIANI WAS FROM Santa Giuletta, whereas Federico Valle was from Asti. They met in a place that was halfway round the world from their relatively adjacent birthplaces in Italy. Valle was born on January 21, 1880 (Figure 4.1).

At the age of 16, he found a job with the representatives of the Italian branch of Société Lumière, and was probably hired by Vittorio Calcina, from Turin, Lumière's general agent and strategist in conquering the peninsula for the *cinématographe*. In 1898, Valle went to Paris to be trained as an operator. Then he travelled as an operator for the Parisian company Urban Trading & Co. (renamed Eclypse in 1906), which allowed him to visit several countries in Europe and Asia Minor. Starting in 1908, he also got to travel extensively to film documentaries in South America—in

CITTA' DI ASTI

UFFICIO DELLO STATO CIVILE

ESTRATTO PER RIASSUNTO DAL REGISTRO DEGLI ATTI DI NASCITA

DELL'ANNO _1880_

Nel registro degli ATTI DI NASCITA di questo Comune dell'anno _1880_

Parte _I_ Serie _—_ Uff. _1_ trovasi iscritto l'atto N. _94_

dal quale risulta che in data _ventuno gennaio mille ottocento ottanta_

alle ore _10_ è nato in questo Comune

Valle Federico Pasquale, Carlo Alberto

da Vittorio e da Capurro Marina

L'atto fu redatto su questi registri coll'osservanza di tutte le formalità di legge.

ANNOTAZIONI

Per estratto conforme all'originale rilasciato

In carta libera per gli usi per il quale la legge non prescrive il bollo

Asti, addì _23 MAG.1981_ 197

L'UFFICIALE DELLO STATO CIVILE

FIGURE 4.1   The birth certificate (from Asti, Italy) of Federico Valle, producer of *El Apóstol*.

Argentina, Uruguay, Paraguay, Brazil, and Peru. In 1909, he did something remarkable when he flew on Wilbur Wright's airplane from the Centocelle Airport in Rome and shot the very first aerial footage in history. He moved to Buenos Aires permanently in 1911, where he opened a small laboratory for developing and printing films that were primarily concerned with inserting

Spanish subtitles in foreign language movies. Right after that, he founded his own production company, Cinematografía Valle, which specialized in documentaries and newsreels. Valle himself shot a lot of footage while travelling in the *Pampas*, Argentina's vast interior.

Therefore, in the 1910s, Valle was one of the few influential young Argentinean filmmakers. The early Argentinean cinema was limited to sporadic presentations, which came, more or less frequently, from the United States (Edison's first kinetoscope in 1894) or from France (the first of Lumière's films was shown in 1896), or from individual small-time entrepreneurs such as Belgian Henri Lapage, who imported newsreels from Europe and sometimes filmed them on-site. Lepage also imported cameras and various cinematographic materials.

The first Argentinean film with actors was *La Revolución de Mayo* (The May Revolution), shown in 1909; the first, although modest, hit was *El fusilamiento de Dorrego*[*] (Dorrego Executed by a Firing Squad, 1910), which was presented to the public by the Italian director Mario Gallo (1877–1945), three years after having immigrated to become a pianist and teacher for opera choir. The movie employed an emphatic style of theatrical acting similar to the style used in some French films of the time, and was a starting point to allow Gallo and others to begin producing new narrative films. Success finally arrived in 1915 when *Nobleza gaucha* (Gaucho Nobility: written and directed by Humberto Cairo in collaboration with Federico Gunche and Eduardo Martinez de la Pera) unanimously won over both the public and the critics, and was also distributed in Brazil and Spain. At middecade, when World War I interrupted the supply of films from European producers, the Argentinean film industry could count on laboratories and studios built in 1909 by Julio Raúl Alsina, plus the production, distribution,

---

[*] Manuel Dorrego (1787–1828) was one of Argentina's—and of independent Latin America's—founding fathers. A controversial figure, he was defeated by coup leader and personal enemy Juan Lavalle and executed.

FIGURE 4.2   Federico Valle during the 1920s, when he was one of the most important Argentinean film producers.

and filmmaking company that belonged to Max Glucksmann (successor of the Lepage company's founder) and the rental company that belonged to Julián de Ajuria (Sociedad general cinematográfica). And naturally, there was also Federico Valle (Figure 4.2).

Valle began developing his natural tendency to make *reportage* films when he started producing the first newsreels in Argentina, the *Actualidades Valle*. His lively weekly updates were shown until 1930, a total of 657 editions.

In a country that was accustomed to political vignettes, a good newsreel had to have a few caricatures, and so Valle decided to find himself a political caricaturist. He chose the young man from Santa Giuletta whose work he had seen published in the newspapers. Cristiani accepted the job; all he had to do was turn in a drawing for the close of the week's newsreel. It was not an animated drawing: the footage showed a hand quickly sketching the drawing and then the drawing that stayed on the screen a few seconds after it was finished. It was a good idea, even though it was not new: at the end of the nineteenth century, this type of drawing had become very popular in Great Britain (it was called a *lightning sketch* and derived from a variety show number in which an entertainer did quick caricatures of members of the audience). Valle had probably seen lightning sketches while he worked as a traveling cameraman, and so he decided to have his new collaborator do something similar. Both Cristiani and Valle realized that a still picture was unnatural for a "moving picture." One day, Valle saw a strange film from France where things moved by themselves, and he thought that if objects could move, then so could drawings. On seeing the footage, Cristiani promised to think about it.

> "In this film, there were matches moving around," remembered Cristiani. "And then I found out that Emile Cohl had made it. I studied it for some time, frame after frame of the entire reel, and I would not rest until I discovered how he had made each of those matches move. I couldn't see any strings. The explanation was that Cohl had painstakingly moved the matches by hand, shooting each frame one at a time. At that time, we didn't make movies with 24 frames per second because we used a hand cranked machine that shot from 14 to 16 frames per second. But even at that rate, it was an enormous job. I took it as a bit of a game, and a bit of a challenge, and decided to try my hand."

After learning the craft, Cristiani immediately began to put it to good use, which inevitably was limited by the circumstances and technology of the era. His first studio was a terrace, chosen because it was in the sun all day long (artificial light, floodlights, and lamps were not common equipment). Following Cohl's example with animated objects, Cristiani created "objects" by cutting shapes out of construction paper, similar to two-dimensional marionettes.

The pieces of his cut-out figures were sewn together at the joints, which allowed him to position them as he liked. The figures were then laid on a horizontal surface set on the terrace floor with a primitive urban camera mounted directly over them. Cristiani moved the figures and then turned the crank, so that the camera shot one frame. A small change of position, and then a turn of the crank, and so on. In addition to the problems of using sunlight and working at a snail's pace, Cristiani also had to kneel while he was working, and therefore had to get up and stretch every so often. On top of that, the wind would occasionally blow the figures out of position, forcing him to start over.

At any rate, he finished the job. *Actualidades Valle* could finally present a moving political caricature, which was (as far as we know today) the very first Argentinean animated film: *La intervención a la provincia de Buenos Aires*. This brief movie was dated 1916 by Argentinean sources, but the date is not confirmed because President Yrigoyen prepared an *intervención* in the April of 1917. Right now, we have no way of knowing for sure, but we can make some guesses. It is reasonable to assume that the president's intentions were evident some time prior to his final actions (in the news and everyday discussion about current events). Everyone knew how about the hostility that the governor of Buenos Aires felt toward the new president since his election in the spring of 1916.

> "It was my first film," remembered Cristiani, "and it was very short—it lasted about one minute. Marcelino Ugarte, the governor, was a short man who always wore a top hat. The film showed a hand holding a hammer with the word *intervención* written on it, and this hammer pounded Ugarte on the head. The top hat was knocked down to completely cover the figure. Actually, the Ugarte administration was not very clean, and so the public really liked this little film."

Almost immediately, Cristiani found himself working from the very short format to the feature length film. The success of the animated drawings caught the attention of Guillermo Franchini, a wealthy businessman who owned the Richmond *confiterías* (tea rooms) and also movie theatres. Cristiani said: "Franchini looked ahead. He asked Valle to go into business with him and agreed to provide the capital. He wanted to make a longer movie of the same type, a political feature film."

This is the story of how the first animated feature film came to be.

The producer hired Alfonso de Laferrère (the 24-year-old son of one of Argentina's most famous playwrights, Gregorio) to write the script. Then he got busy with the production process. He asked Cristiani if he felt like animating and directing the film, and Cristiani said he would, but that he needed some help because the job was long and meticulous. Propelled by his enthusiasm and encouraged by Franchini's financial support, Valle hired Andrés Ducaud (architect and scenographer), who was entrusted with the job of building three-dimensional models of the main monuments in Buenos Aires. Valle also recruited into the adventure the Peruvian journalist and scenographer José Bustamante y Ballivián, his most trusted collaborator. And finally, Franchini asked Valle to contact the most famous caricaturist of the era, Diógenes "El Mono" Taborda. However, Taborda's contribution was not as important as many thought, then and later.

REFERENCES

Cairo, H., F. Gunche, and E. M. de la Pera. (1915). *Nobleza gaucha.*
Cristiani, Q. (1916). *La intervención a la provincia de Buenos Aires.*
Gallo, M. (1909). *La Revolución de Mayo.*
Gallo, M. (1910). *El fusilamiento de Dorrego.*

CHAPTER 5

Taborda, Cristiani, and *El Apóstol*

H ISTORIANS OF ARGENTINEAN CARICATURES define Diógenes Taborda as a "gran dibujante," "gran humorista," and "joven bohemio lleno de talento."* He was born in Concordia (in the province of Entre Ríos) in 1890, and he died in Mendoza on June 3, 1926. He drew vignettes, illustrations, and caricatures about political themes and popular customs of the people of Buenos Aires. He had become the most famous pencil in the afternoon paper *Crítica*, founded in 1913 by Natalio Botana. Capable of summarizing the current political situation clearly and concisely, he created a short but legendary series: *Hípicas*, in which he used the literal meaning of popular horse race jargon matched with illustrations of situations with a completely different meaning. The *Hípicas* were so successful that they spawned an independent magazine. In Argentina, Diógenes Taborda was immensely popular. He was the first caricaturist, and remains the only one, to be honored with a street in the capital city named after him.

---

* Great draftsman, Great humorist, Young bohemian full of talent.

His style was similar to that of cartoonists as he used balloons for character dialog, and influenced most of the best of the country's budding colleagues. Fellow journalists nicknamed Taborda "El Mono," that is "The Monkey" ("because he was really ugly!" said Cristiani). From then on, or maybe we should say, from his time on, caricatures and vignettes are known *monos* in Argentina, and *pintamonos* was the name for the caricaturist or (in a negative sense) an artist who does not produce "serious" art or is not very talented.

And so, Taborda met with Franchini, Valle, and Cristiani. He loved the idea of bringing his caricatures to life on the screen, and the compensation offered made him even more enthusiastic. He started his work and presented Cristiani with a few sketches.

Cristiani was dismayed. "His drawings were very good, but how could I animate them? They were rigid, and also very detailed. Excellent static drawings, but they were not created for animated cinema."

Taborda quickly tired of the movie making project. The enormous amount of work scared him, and he did not have the discipline necessary for the slow, patient process of shooting the film, given his free-spirited personality.

Cristiani and Taborda were both colleagues and good friends. One was discovering the film industry and wanted to do it his way, and the other had the best of intentions to get out of a situation that was not as great as he had first thought. And so they made a deal. In Cristiani's words:

> "I asked Taborda if he would be upset if I modified his drawings, to make them simpler but without losing the quality of his style. He answered in a friendly way that, since I was the specialist, I could do what I thought was necessary for my job. And that he was really only

interested in seeing his name in the opening credits. That's how it went. So, with Valle's permission, Taborda was billed as the 'creator of the characters.' The truth—and I'm saying this without trying to get all the credit—is that I did the drawing work, including the creation of the other characters in the movie. His character of Yrigoyen was an excellent but grotesque caricature, and we really were supposed to portray him as a 'holy apostle,' that is, as a pleasing character" (Figures 5.1 and 5.2).

FIGURE 5.1 Preliminary drawing by Diógenes ("El Mono") Taborda for *El Apóstol*. Hipólito Yrigoyen is shown with the symbols of power, slippers (denoting the middle class), and the boina blanca (the white beret) that was an emblem of the Radical party.

FIGURE 5.2 Preliminary drawing by Diógenes ("El Mono") Taborda for *El Apóstol*. Yrigoyen and José Cantilo Crotto, a popular senator and later a governor of Buenos Aires. Of Italian–Argentinean descent, Crotto is depicted as half gaucho and half peasant immigrant.

However, "El Mono" could not resist the temptation to say what he thought about the animated drawings. Here is what he wrote about them:

> Animated drawings are a ground-breaking development. They are about to become the next "crusade" of art on film, since they make it possible to create funny films, which is their best characteristic. Our "characters" are up

against the likes of Charlie Chaplin and Max Linder on the screen, and their hilarious antics bring a smile to the faces of even the most apathetic spectators. I guarantee it, absolutely.

We do not know how many months it took to shoot *El Apóstol* (this was the title chosen for the film). We do know, however, that the production process was extraordinarily quick, and Cristiani was destined to become known for his speed in the years to come. Normally, animation requires lengthy production times, even if teams are well trained and specialized, but this film was made by a bunch of newcomers—the most expert of which was Cristiani who had only a one-minute film to his credit. It is clear that the animation techniques that he used were not the extremely elaborate processes that were being used during the same period in France and the United States. In addition, animation of cut-out figures can be done more simply than when using paper or cel.* The process took an amazingly short time, and on November 9, 1917 *El Apóstol* "opened" at the Cine Select-Suipacha, in calle Suipacha 482. In the best of estimates, Cristiani and his team had worked for less than 10 months to shoot the 1700 meters of film, its special effects and 58,000 phases of animation. The film lasted 60–70 minutes (Figure 5.3).

From a technical point of view, *El Apóstol* meant a giant leap forward from *Intervención*. Filming had been done indoors with artificial light, at the studio Talleres Cinematográficos Valle, located in calle Reconquista 452. Cristiani himself had set up the artificial lighting, an arrangement of batteries and carbon rods to

---

* A cel is a sheet of transparent celluloid. Before digital technologies took over, phases of character movement were painted on these sheets.

FIGURE 5.3 An advertising flyer of *El Apóstol*.

create primitive voltaic arc lamps. He had even perfected his technique of animating jointed cut-out figures.

> "If I was working with a human figure, I had to separate it into independent drawings: head, body, arm, forearm, hand, fingers, legs, feet, etc. Then I sewed them together, tying knots to link the parts together and form the figure. In this way, the figure could be made to do any movement I wanted. I filmed these cut-out, sewn-together figures personally, because that is where creativity was actually expressed, through humor and perfect animation."

Cristiani patented this technique with Argentina Patent n. 15,498 of the year 1917.

REFERENCE

Cristiani, Q. (1917). *El Apóstol*.

CHAPTER 6

The First Feature Length Animated Film in History

THE FIRST IMAGES OF *El Apóstol* graced the screen at the Cine Select-Suipacha (owned by the film's financer, Guillermo Franchini) on November 9, 1917. A ticket cost two pesos.

"It was a very prestigious theater," remembered Quirino Cristiani almost 70 years later, with a note of reverence in his voice.

The plot was fairly linear, even if a few subplots made it slightly complicated. It showed Hipólito Yrigoyen lying on a plain cot (the president was known for his sober lifestyle), tossing and turning because of the moral decadence of the Argentinean people. Finally, he falls asleep and another figure, his spirit, detaches from the sleeping body and goes up to Olympus. He is dressed as an apostle: the apostle of national redemption. On his arrival, he speaks energetically with the gods, describing the deeds and misdeeds of the *porteños*, explaining that too many people still laugh at his political programs and at him as well. His speech provides the context for a long scene in which a few congressmen take the floor to express their positions, whereas other characters refer to the level of chaos in the capital city's administration. Still others debate financial problems, mainly the government's debts. At last, with the fiery zeal of a man who wants to change the nation, Yrigoyen asks Zeus to give him lightning bolts to strike the corrupt Buenos Aires and purify it with a vast fire. The god grants his request. The main buildings in the city are hit by lightning, and are consumed in the huge fire. This marks the beginning of a brave new world: the current Sodom is destroyed and Yrigoyen builds a novel city, a symbol of a novel nation, from its ashes. But naturally, it was only a dream: the head of the radical faction, now head of the government, reawakens in his bed. From now on, he will have to fight all kinds of real difficulties that he had never before imagined.

The most impressive scene was the destruction of Buenos Aires. It was made with the use of several three-dimensional models built by architect Andrés Ducaud. One was 10 meters wide, and portrayed a view of the city from the river bank, with ships anchored in the harbor. There were also other smaller models of the Congress building, the city hall (the Municipalidad), and the Obras Santiarias sports club. Finally, there was a model of the center of town with stoplights, store signs, and moving automobiles. So many precise details amazed spectators in 1917. The scene was then rendered horrific by the *efectos fotográficos*, which were probably superimposed flames with a red tone (for the fire) and a blue tone (for the floods).

Jorge Miguel Couselo made this statement about the film's historical and political impact:

> The old regime—conservatism, the oligarchy, the "lying, faithless regime" that Yrigoyen attacked verbally—put the new winner on guard against the risks of power, the vain

illusion of drastic changes, the deceptive dream of waking the nation from a long period of apathy. The film's main character was lampooned without pity, as if he were much more influential than is actually true. The apostle was a presumptuous clay-footed giant incapable of attracting the support of the "infidels" and presumed enemies of the country. At the same time, everyone else was humorously ridiculed, including the former opposition members now in government positions and former governors who had passed over to the opposition but without accepting the loss of power.

The newspapers published openly favorable reviews. *Crítica* wrote:

> It's a magnificent film subject, and it again demonstrates how much progress being made in our national film industry ... It's exquisite satire.

La Nación:

> The 58,000 drawings can sustain comparison with the finest American movies in this category, without being judged inferior.

La Razón praised the "long, patient graphic work that showed much originality" and remarked that:

> The *porteño* audience laughed at its politicians as it used to, years ago. Today, collective humor has a more modern process, the animated drawing, to express its inoffensive malevolence.

A specialized film publication, the weekly *La Película*, published two articles. The one published before the film that came out contained an antiquated comparison of an animated cinema and *Aesop's fables*, with a biting and equally outdated comparison of political versus fairy-tail animals. The second article commented on the movie's success, with particular praise for the aforementioned fire scene. In this issue, they added:

> The presentation of the film with moving drawings [*sic*] *El Apóstol* [represented] a great film event, accompanied by repeated success at each new showing at the Select.

Less enthusiastic, 43 years later, the historian Domingo di Núbila wrote in his *Historia del cine argentino*:

> The inevitable imprecision of the first work in the field of animated drawings, *El Apóstol* did not enjoy as much success as could reward the labor that went into making it.

Di Núbila certainly never saw the film since it quickly disappeared from the marquis and was later lost in the fire at the Valle studios in 1926, but he was both right and wrong about the movie's success.

The public actually loved it. The theater manager had to replace the single program, which consisted in a main feature accompanied by other less important works of different types, with a cyclical program in which the main film was shown several times during the same day, as happens now in today's theatres. At first, *El Apóstol* was paired with another film, and then it became the main attraction. It was on the marquis for more than six months, being shown seven times per day. The financial results were satisfying both for Franchini and Valle, who continued to produce animated films, as we will see later on.

On the other hand, the movie was not *widely* successful, and appealed to a small portion of the population. It was strictly for a Buenos Aires audience: nobody in the provinces even saw it because it was not distributed there. And likewise, given the subject, it was not possible to export the film to other nations, not even to a close cousin similar to Uruguay.

Cristiani got both roses and thorns from the project. After such a mammoth job, he was paid a mere 1000 pesos, a small sum even at that time, and his name appeared in miniscule print in the opening credits. But on the other hand, he had learned a trade, patented an invention, and people were finding out who had really done all the work on that movie, which was good for new professional possibilities. Moreover, he had another reason to be happy, which was completely unrelated to his work: On September 1, 1917, with Diógenes Taborda as his best man, Quirino Cristiani got married.

REFERENCES

Aesop. (1921–1929). *Aesop's fables.*
Cristiani, Q. (1917). *El Apóstol.*
di Núbila, D. (1960). *Historia del cine argentino.*

CHAPTER 7

The Cristiani Family

IT ALL STARTED DURING the carnival in 1916. Cocoliche was a character that represented a Neapolitan immigrant, with funny-looking patched clothes and grammatically incorrect sayings that had quickly filtered into everyday conversation from the play *Juan Moreira*.* It was the perfect costume for a creative young man who still was not sure he was going to make any money in his lifetime. All he had to do was find a few old garments and act a little strange. During his carnival outings, Cristiani (then 20) went through the Parque Patricios neighborhood, near the Boca where the population was mainly made up of Italians, as it is today also.†

---

* In 1884, actor and playwright José Podestá adapted for the stage the namesake novel by Eduardo Gutiérrez, with enormous success. This was the beginning of the national Argentinean theater.

† About 25% of the inhabitants of Buenos Aires were Italian at that time. "The Argentinean atmosphere is filled with Italianism," exclaimed Luigi Einaudi, who became the second president of the Italian Republic in 1948. And Jorge Luis Borges's grandmother, who did not realize how big the immigrant population was, commented unhappily, "these Italians are dying all the time!" as she read the obituaries of more and more people with Italian surnames. The Italians on the Rio de la Plata were not poor similar to those living on the Hudson or in the Brazilian *facendas*, where they were hired to replace the blacks after slavery was abolished (1888). The Banco de Italia y Rio de la Plata has existed since 1871.

On the front porch of a house in Parque Patricios stood Celina Cordara, then 15 years old and very pretty. Cristiani stared at her without knowing what to do. He was shy and had never had a girlfriend, so he was at a loss for words. On top of all that, he was wearing that ridiculous Cocoliche costume that made him look even more awkward. Celina's mother peeked out of the door, and commented mercilessly on what she saw in the Lombard dialect: "El par un tarlücc!" ("He looks like an idiot!").

Despite this disastrous beginning, the two young people became friends and their affection for one another grew. Quirino began to make a little more money, and was able to improve his wardrobe. To tell the truth, he followed the same fads as the other *bohemios* and became quite a dandy. He began visiting Celina Cordara dressed in a top hat and a yellow vest with a cane and spats. His only problem was that her neighborhood often flooded because Parque Patricios is located where the small river Riachuelo empties into the Rio de la Plata. Thus,

---

In 1887, the Nuevo Banco Italiano opened and in 1898, the Banco Popular Italiano opened. Italians owned 36% of the real estate, against 42% owned by Argentineans and 22% by other foreigners. They rapidly became a class of small industry owners and merchants, furniture craftsmen, and construction contractors. The upper middle class was present: the Vasena family (metalworking industry), the Canale family (food industry), and the Vaccari family (matches and printing). Naturally, there was also another side of the coin: poverty, exploitation, and marginalization. But the Italians suffered less in Argentina than in almost any other country. In addition, integration was easy since the customs and language were similar to those in their mother country. New arrivals easily morphed into *Criollos*. There were many associations: labor unions, cultural circles, patriotic organizations, recreational circles, and charities—and other groups performed several of these functions simultaneously. In 1904, there were 86 associations in Buenos Aires alone, with 48,946 members (a comprehensive figure, but some people belonged to more than one association). Finally, there were also newspapers. Between 1887 and the beginning of the 1900s, there were over twenty Italian language daily newspapers (including the *Provincia Pavese*) and another 20 publications, which came out weekly, biweekly, or monthly.

young Quirino had occasionally to reach his beloved's house with a bouquet of flowers in one hand and his shoes and socks in the other, and his elegant trousers rolled up to his knees and wrinkled. When the waters were particularly high and he could not get home, he had to find somewhere in the vicinity to sleep. And since it was unacceptable at that time for a young suitor to sleep under the same roof as his darling, he had to settle for a hard billiard table in a nearby bar in order to sleep somewhere dry.

The wedding was held on September 1, 1917 and the couple had two sons: (1) Luis Quirino (1918–1975) and (2) Atilio Leopoldo (1919–2004). The elder son had a daughter, Gracia, and she also went on to have a daughter, Maria de los Angeles. The younger son had two sons: Héctor Osvaldo and Jorge. Quirino Cristiani's father-in-law was an Italian from Mortara, and his mother-in-law, Luisa Aduna, was Basque but had learned the Lombard dialect perfectly. Future generations of the Cristiani family attribute their stubbornness to her and her lineage. In fact, the Basques tend to be proud of their headstrong nature.

Family life was destined to be harmonious and serene. Luis Quirino later became an animator in his father's studio, and Atilio Leopoldo also worked with him, though not as an artist.

The floods did not cease to be part of their domestic lives. Years later, when the boys were older, the family would spend weekends at Olivos camping on the beach and sleeping in a tent. One Saturday night, the river turned against Quirino Cristiani once more. A flash flood forced them to quickly gather their things and provisions. Mrs. Cristiani and their sons were able to collect their stuff without too many problems, but the director reacted more calmly (maybe more sleepily). He put on his shirt, tie, and jacket and walked out in his underwear carrying the rest of his clothing as if it were the most natural thing in the world. He finished dressing on the station platform while waiting for the train that would take them home, complaining about the stroke of bad luck but unembarrassed about his appearance. He was, after all, a nudist.

In November 1983, the magazine *Humor* published an interview with Cristiani, then 87, written by the artist Eduardo Ferro. Here is what he had to say about the subject of nudism.

> I founded the very first naturist-nudist association in Argentina. We bought an island in the Delta [of Rio de la Plata] and named it Heliopolis, the City of the Sun. The story went like this: I was collaborating with *Última Hora*, and the director allowed me to publish a message free of charge in which I asked to make contact with naturists, and I invited them to a meeting in my laboratory. Over twenty people showed up. One of the ladies in the group was very rich, and she let us use her house in Ituzaingó, which had a vast park for us to meet in. At our first gathering, there were twenty-five nude people. [...] Then we bought the island and build two shelters that we later turned into dressing rooms. We didn't want our behavior to look like a *strip-tease*. [...] I can even tell you about a day that my wife came with me, and she did not want to take off her clothing. Everyone had no trouble accepting that she preferred to wear a bathing suit.

REFERENCE

Gutiérrez, E. (1880). *Juan Moreira*.

CHAPTER 8

Sin Dejar Rastro

ON April 4, 1917 the small merchant ship *Monte Protegido* was sunk by "unknown" submarines.

Argentina had remained neutral since the beginning of the World War I. When he became president, Yrigoyen had tried to balance the affinities with the English and French held by the majority of the population* and the armed forces' propensity toward Germany, with whom they shared the same type of army, mentality, and training.

Even though South America was a secondary realm of operations, both the Allies and the Axis would have liked to gain Argentina's support, and not only because Brazil had sided with Great Britain. Argentina was a rich source of food, and the Germans and Austrians were going to be desperately in need of provisions during the last months of the war.

The sinking of the *Monte Protegido* was not clear from the start. It was almost certain that the Germans were behind it, in an attempt to throw the blame on the English and sway public opinion,

---

* A strange Argentinean tradition was that it was a Spanish-speaking country that traded with England and sent its children to study in Paris.

so that Argentina would side with Germany. Yrigoyen demanded an explanation from the imperial government and obtained an account of the facts and reimbursement for damages. In September, secret dispatches made by the German ambassador to Buenos Aires, Count von Luxburg, were discovered. It was a serious incident: The president asked the ambassador to leave Argentina immediately and the German government lost no time in sending further explanations and renouncing von Luxburg's work entirely. Yrigoyen's stubborn anti-war, anti-military stance caused the air to clear and Argentina remained neutral. Obviously, the citizens of Buenos Aires talked about the event for months, and it was the subject of comments, interpretations, and speculations of all sorts.

It was the perfect subject for another movie such as *El Apóstol*.

Quirino Cristiani was not satisfied with what Federico Valle had paid him for the first film, and he also was not happy about the producer interfering considerably in his work (assigning unwanted collaborators, giving little relevance to his name in the opening credits). It was a relief to be called by the entrepreneur Della Valle y Fauvety with a new proposal. Della Valle y Fauvety was president of Gath y Chaves, a famous departmental store in Buenos Aires. He was fiercely anti-German, and asked Cristiani to make a new feature film, in the same style as the first, about the episode concerning Count von Luxburg. He promised the director all the artistic and organizational freedom he wanted. Cristiani accepted the proposal and started the new film right after he finished shooting *El Apóstol*. Toward the middle of 1918, the new film was ready to be presented to the public. It was based on a screenplay by José Bayoni, and its title was *Sin dejar rastro* (Without Leaving a Trace) (Figure 8.1).

"It was a funny film in which I told about this event in a comical way, and ridiculed the Prussian ambassador. It was also a very courageous film because international politics was an even touchier subject than internal politics, and I managed to retain my irreverence without watering it down," said Cristiani.

FIGURE 8.1   An advertising flyer of *Sin dejar rastro.*

The authorities did not appreciate such boldness, and this time they intervened drastically. *Sin dejar rastro* was shown to the public for only one day at the theater Select-Lavalle. The following day, the copies and negative were confiscated. The reason for such an action: the episode was over and done with and stirring up public opinion would have meant new tension between the two governments and also new difficulties.

The movie was never seen again after it was confiscated. Like the sunken ship, it disappeared without leaving a trace.

> "This title says nothing to today's movie-goers," said Quirino Cristiani, "but it was very clear for yesterday's spectators. Everyone knew that Count von Luxburg had organised that incident. He had given instructions by telegram to naval commanders and wanted them to act in secret 'without leaving a trace' of themselves. The actual phrase was *spurlos versenkt*, which was immediately translated into 'sin dejar rastro'" which became a saying, almost a proverb. There were no victims of the incident, and the survivors provided enough evidence to draw the conclusion that the German navy was responsible for it after all."

REFERENCES

Cristiani, Q. (1917). *El Apóstol*.
Cristiani, Q. (1918). *Sin dejar rastro*.

---

* In truth, the German phrase should be translated more precisely as *sunk without a trace* or *sunk without leaving a trace*.

CHAPTER 9

Early Animation and the Feature Film

A T THE END OF 1917, Quirino Cristiani had directed the first animated feature length film in movie history, and a year later, Argentina could also boast about its quantity as well: three animated features, two by Cristiani and one by Andrés Ducaud (actually four, if we count Ducaud's second work, *La Carmen criolla*, made with animated puppets) (Figure 9.1).[*]

It needs to be understood that making a feature length film in the field of animated cinema is not (and never has been) simply a question of working harder and investing more money than would normally be necessary for a short film. This is true when speaking of live-action movies. The language in animated films tends to be concise by nature, and therefore a feature length work becomes difficult artistically and with regard to rhythm. In addition, animated cinema was originally done by artists and artisans, either alone or in small groups in tiny studios. Therefore, the work did not involve using large quantities of stock, financing several weeks of filming, or paying actors for many months. It was a matter of

---

[*] Ducaud's feature films are discussed in Appendix 4.

FIGURE 9.1   An image of *La Carmen criolla* (or *Una noche de gala en el Colón*), a film made by the background artist of *El Apóstol*, Andrés Ducaud.

drawing on thousands of sheets of paper, filming thousands of photograms one by one, and producing the entire work by hand.

On this basis, it is not strange that very few animated feature length films were produced before the computer became a common tool: a mere handful compared to the number of live-action films, and a tiny percentage if compared with the number of short animated films. The few Argentinean feature films of 1917–1918 were the only ones of their kind until about 1940, except for *The Adventures of Prince Achmed* (directed by Lotte Reiniger, Germany 1926); *Peludópolis* (directed by Quirino Cristiani, Argentina 1931); *The New Gulliver* (directed by Aleksandr Ptushko, USSR 1935); *Snow White and the Seven Dwarves* (directed by David Hand and produced by Walt Disney, USA 1937); *The Golden Key* (directed by Aleksandr Ptushko, USSR 1939); *Gulliver's Travels* (directed by Dave Fleischer, USA 1939).

In Latin America, Cristiani and his colleagues were not only the people to make feature length animated films, but even the only ones to do animation. Based on current information, there was only one other South American animator, Seth in Brazil, who had a few things in common with Cristiani. Seth (his real name was Alvaro Marins) was a well-known caricaturist from Rio de Janeiro who published his drawings in a newspaper, *A Noite*, and who decided to make a political propaganda film. He called it *O Kaiser*, and used it to poke fun at the emperor of Germany, William II (at the time, Brazil was at war with Germany and Austria–Hungary, alongside the Allies).

Similar to *El Apóstol*, *O Kaiser* also came out in 1917, but only ran for two days: from January 22 to the 24.

It was a very short film that showed the Kaiser and a globe that did not want him to dominate it. The stubborn globe got bigger and bigger until it swallowed the Kaiser. After this film, Seth made a few animated works for advertising purposes.*

Up until the 1920s, animated cinema was very much in an embryonic stage. After being created simultaneously in both France and the United States around 1908/1909, it developed slowly in these two countries over the following decade (in America, *animated cartoons* rivaled live comedy routines, and brought some famous comic strip characters from national newspaper strips to the big screen). In Germany, the United Kingdom, Spain, and Russia there were a few isolated artists or some small studios that focused mainly on advertising or special effects. This overall panorama of the field of animation during those years shows just how special those first films were. Argentinean animators were courageous and way ahead of their time, and so were producers such as Valle and Franchini and other financers that believed in this new form of expression.

From a more critical point of view, since it is impossible to evaluate those films that are now lost or missing, it is important to

---

* Brazil could count on a few isolated pioneers, scattered here and there in its history, until the 1950s when Anelio Latini Filho dared to embark on a project for making a feature length film (*Sinfonia Amazônica*, 1953).

understand the concept of animated film that Quirino Cristiani created at the beginning, and that he continued to develop throughout his career (the only justified exception being *El Mono Relojero*). Cristiani's art was modern and lively; he was not a twentieth-century Aesop who narrated illustrated fairy tales for children. He was a satirical commentator, a vignettist who used moving images to communicate with his public, which rivaled that of daily newspapers. Thanks to his rapid work, he was always able to nail down the day's news and highlight the comical, joyful, or the ridiculous. This type of cinema had no "artistic" ambition; it was the movie of a columnist with a pencil, such as Jules Feiffer. According to the director and a few witnesses living at the time the first draft of this book was written, this type of movie was talkative, simple, and clever—and was definitely made for adults. The children's fairy-tale, destined to become synonymous with animation because of Disney's work, did not attract the Argentinean director until 1938.

At that time, though, "political" animation was not only made in Argentina. In addition to Brazil, animated war propaganda films were also shown in Great Britain and the United States. We must remember the *Sinking of the Lusitania* by the American Winsor McCay, who also created the comic strip *Little Nemo in Slumberland*, and was a pioneer in animated movies. Greatly moved by the tragic sinking of the transatlantic ocean liner by a German submarine (on May 7, 1915: 1198 civilians drowned, 124 were Americans), he produced this medium length film, a jewel of creative graphics and cinematography. The film was presented to the public on July 20, 1918. "The film attracted attention due to its length, not because it was a war propaganda film," wrote the historian Earl Theisen in 1933.* In addition to the theme similar to *Sin dejar rastro* (also about a sunken ship),

---

* Mentioned in John Canemaker, *Winsor McCay*, Retrospectives catalogue, Zagreb, 5th World Festival of Animated Films, 1982.

the *Sinking of the Lusitania* is mentioned in this book because for years it was considered to be a "long" film, due to what spectators remembered (and thus wrongly identified as a feature length film), and also wrongly considered to be the first feature length animated film in history.*

REFERENCES

Canemaker, J. (1987). *Winsor McCay*.
Cristiani, Q. (1917). *El Apóstol*.
Cristiani, Q. (1918). *Sin dejar rastro*.
Cristiani, Q. (1931). *Peludópolis*.
Cristiani, Q. (1938). *El Mono Relojero*.
Ducaud, A. (1918). *La Carmen criolla*.
Filho, L. (1953). *Sinfonia Amazônica*.
Fleischer, D. (1939). *Gulliver's travels*.
Hand, D. (Director) and Walt Disney (Producer). (1937). *Snow white and the seven dwarves*.
Marins, A. (1917). *O Kaiser*.
McCay, W. (1905). *Little Nemo in Slumberland*.
McCay, W. (1918). *Sinking of the Lusitania*.
Ptushko, A. (1935). *The new Gulliver*.
Ptushko, A. (1939). *The golden key*.
Reiniger, L. (1926). *The adventures of Prince Achmed*.
Tait, C. (1906). *The story of the Kelly Gang*.

---

* A bit of trivia: according to the history books, the first live-action feature film in history was the Australian film *The Story of the Kelly Gang*, directed by Charles Tait in 1906. Length 1219 meters, duration 60–70 minutes. Therefore, the southern hemisphere holds the record for the first feature length films in both categories—live action and animation.

CHAPTER 10

Federico Valle

FEDERICO VALLE, IN HIS day, was one of the biggest film producers in the world. In addition to everything mentioned here so far, he also promoted a series of animated scientific films and at least one of those (*The marvelous world of insects*) was made by Cristiani. But his career was not limited to the field of animation or to newsreels. He produced more than a thousand documentaries and industrial films, as well as several narrative movies. His first was *El ovillo fatal* (*The Fatal Ball*, directed by Matilde Caro, 1917); and in 1922 he made *Milonguita* (the *milonga* is a popular folk dance), written and directed by the same collaborator involved in *El Apóstol*, José Bustamante y Ballivián. In addition, in 1922, Valle presented three feature length narrative films set in beautiful but little known areas of southern Argentina: *Patagonia!*, *Jangada florida*, and *Allá en el Sur*.

Once Valle decided to send one of his collaborators, Arnold Etchebehere, to the southern province of Chubut. The exact location was the mountain towns of El Bolson and Esquel, on the Andes near the Chilean border. They were shooting in scenic areas where the landscape was breathtaking and relatively unknown to the movie-going public, who were mostly city dwellers.

In addition, he had included a young actor in the project, Arauco Randal, whom he had discovered, along with Nelo Cosimi, an Italian-born theater star who later became a director and scenographer. Between filming in Chubut and the "joiners" shot in the studio, the three docufiction works cost a total of 22,000 pesos, and they made him a lot more.

Another of Valle's ideas was to put Angel Luis Firpo in front of the camera. The boxer had become famous after his quest for the world heavyweight title (as we will see later, Cristiani was also interested in Firpo). The movie was titled *El toro salvaje de las pampas* ("The wild bull of the *pampas*" was the boxer's nickname). It contained lots of actual footage of boxing matches, some authentic shots from the film *Revista Valle* newsreels, and other scenes that were staged for the occasion. The plot was a tearjerker story about a boxer who returns to the ring when his young son needs expensive medicine. The director was Carlo Campogalliani (1885–1974), born in Modena, Italy, who would return to Italy in the 1930s and enjoy a successful career.

Valle unfortunately lost all his equipment in a fire in 1926.* It was a heavy blow, because he was not even insured. However, he continued his work, and in 1928 he presented *Entre los hielos de las islas Orcadas* (Amid the Ice on the Orcadi Islands). He had finished this project before the fire, and he had trained Juan Carlos Moneta, a member of the Argentinean observatory of those distant, ice-packed Antarctic islands, to use the camera. The first version of the film had been completed just a few hours before the fire turned it to ashes. Moneta remarked, "Bah! Another year on the Orcadi Islands!," shouldered his camera and did it all over again.

Valle was ready for the arrival of sound films. He was already experimenting with synchronization through disks. He hired

---

* One of the many fires in the history of early cinema: the film used at that time was celluloid nitrate, and it was highly flammable. The problem was solved in the 1950s when acetate was introduced.

Eduardo Morera to direct a series of short films sung and inter-preted by Carlos Gardel*: *Añoranzas* (Nostalgia), *Canchero* (The Show-off), *Enfundá la mandolina* (Put the Guitar Away), *Mano a mano* (Even), *Rosas de otoño* (Autumn Roses), *Viejo smoking* (Old Tuxedo), *Tengo miedo* (I'm Afraid), and *Yira yira* (Turn around).

The last film produced by Valle was *El drama del collar* (The Drama of the Necklace, 1930), directed by Arturo S. Mom and José Bustamante y Ballivián. Financial difficulties came soon after, as a direct consequence of the military coup of September 6, 1930. After deposing Hipólito Yrigoyen (during his second term as president), the new governors canceled his projects for devel-oping education that had been implemented by the radical gov-ernment. Valle had invested all his money in a program for financing educational films and could not help but surrender. He tried to sell what was left of his archives to the museums, but found no buyers. He did the math, sold the films to a comb fac-tory that melted them down to use them as raw materials, and then he went to live in the Córdoba mountains. The government finally remembered him in 1958, and entrusted him with an assignment at the Instituto nacional de la cinematografía. The same year he reopened communication with the world of cinema by visiting the Mar del Plata film festival, amazed and disheveled (Figure 10.1).

Some of the best directors of the first 30 years of Argentinean cinema learned the ropes at Valle's side. Managing the camera as an aid during the making of *La intervención a la provincia de Buenos Aires* was José Luis Moglia Barth, who in 1934 directed *Riachuelo*, one of the most successful films ever made by the Argentinean film industry. The scenographer of *Riachuelo* was

---

* Carlos Gardel, a handsome tenor who quickly became a living legend of the tango, began his film career in 1917 with a small part in *Flor de durazno* (*Peach Blossoms*, directed by Francisco Defilippis Novoa). He soon moved to Paris and then to Hollywood, to work for Paramount. He was born in 1887, and he died in Colombia in 1935 in a plane crash. Though he is still one of Argentina's fundamental cultural icons, he was either of French or Uruguayan origin. For more information, see Barsky and Barsky (2004).

FIGURE 10.1   Federico Valle, not much time before his death, photographed at the Mar del Plata festival.

Valle's faithful collaborator José Bustamante y Ballivián. Another excellent journalist and scenographer was Chas De Cruz, and the photography directors were Juan, Arnold, and Alberto Etchebehere. Last but not least, Andrés Ducaud and Cristiani were also involved. This is what Cristiani remembered of the first man he worked for in the film industry.

> Valle had a habit of shooting in the remotest interior regions of the country. In fact, this was his most profitable activity. He would send a cameraman and crew to the villages, along with an expert in public relations. This person would then make contact with the village officials

who had to authorize filming in their town, and the footage would later be shown locally. After that phase, the best scenes would be inserted in the *Actualidades Valle*, which were shown all over the country. Naturally, the film had to be financed by the city administration (and started with a close-up of the senior official, his family, and his hierarchical personnel: who could refuse something like that?). The same crew then filmed village festivals, picturesque sights, natural landscapes, factories, and shops (which also contributed money to the project). Many years passed and finally a few journalists from Córdoba found "don Federico," elderly and defeated, "a long way from the noise" in the city of Carlos Paz, the final, quiet destination of all pioneers.*

---

* Federico Valle died in 1960; he was in his eighties. Victor A. Iturralde Rúa, film critic and experimental director, wrote this obituary for him: "I met grandfather two years ago at Mar del Plata. Two long years. Two years of threats and frowns. With the phoenix of crisis, which regularly appeared every six months. With the gray wall of frustration. With printed discourse on stamped paper. With the secretary-director-president of an Institute that stands in for the president-secretary-director. With the empty eyelets of the scissors. Of censorship. I met grandfather two years ago. And I saw him contemplate the rounds. The unchanging, tired, mediocre scene. Journalists, directors, film stars, the man with the smock and the paperwork on their rounds. The noisy, foot-shuffling rounds. Those meaningless rounds, over and over again. And grandfather watched. When I met him, he was already the grandfather. Like many, I didn't know it. And he forgave me, and many others, of our ignorance. Because he was already the grandfather. Because he had already seen many rounds and many grandchildren and he also had been afraid of the phoenix sometimes. And he had hit his head on the wall of frustration. I met him along with another grandfather, who denied his condition. He escaped modesty with his words, with his tremendous *Napoleón*, with his gray hair. He was uneasy in his green suit and for the story. I met him along with Abel Gance. I stayed with the grandfather. His work-worn hands, weathered face, Italian beard, thin unruly hair, calm gestures, absolute simplicity of a grandfather visiting his grandchildren and their friends, his slow voice. A year ago, he returned to the same place and watched the rounds for the last time. Maybe he smiled. Maybe he sighed. Eighty years. Too many, perhaps. Slowly, in silent dialogue with a million pictures, he left for the gateway to peace. And he entered in." *Tiempo de cine*, year I, n. 4, Buenos Aires, November–December 1960, p. 27.

REFERENCES

Barsky, J. and Barsky, O. (2004). *Gardel La biografía*. Taurus, Buenos Aires.

Barth, J. L. M. (1934). *Riachuelo*.

Caro, M. (1917). *El ovillo fatal*.

Cristiani, Q. *The marvelous world of insects*.

Cristiani, Q. (1916). *La intervención a la provincia de Buenos Aires*.

Novoa, F. D. (1917). *Flor de durazno*.

Valle, F. (1928). *Entre los hielos de las islas Orcadas*.

Valle, F. (1930). *El drama del collar*.

CHAPTER 11

Sports, Satire, and Science in Short Films of the 1920s

Italian–British director Gabriele Zucchelli, while researching for his excellent documentary about Quirino Cristiani (2008), was able to find a satirical film two minutes long titled *Los que ligan* (The Ones Who Tie Up) made in 1919 by Cinematografia Valle with animation by Cristiani. It is a humoristic comment on the positions of England, Germany, France, and Argentina after postwar sanctions were imposed by the League of Nations. This film is important because it gives us an idea of the type of satire that Cristiani created for Federico Valle's newsreels, and also because it proves that the two pioneers continued to work together after *El Apóstol*.

The 1920s were very busy for the vignettist/filmmaker. He renewed collaborations with several newspapers and made shorts. Unfortunately, we do not have an exact list of these works with their production dates, unless they were directly related to news or important events. In that case, we can indicate the year.

Depending on the specific case, films were usually on one or two reels without a predetermined duration. Unlike American films, which had very precise time limits (many comedians had to adapt to the passage from the slapstick *one reel* to the more structured, narrative style of *two reels* used in Hollywood between the 1910s and the 1920s), Argentinean films granted more freedom. "These films were sometimes presented after the newsreel," explained Cristiani, "and sometimes, the shorter ones were shown as a prologue to the day's feature. Other times, they were shown during intermission."

First, we should mention the two films about Angel Luis Firpo. This boxer, who stood 195 cm tall (about 6′4″) and weighed 100 kg (about 220 lbs), quickly became the favorite of local fans and then of the American press, which was desperately seeking a rival for the undisputed world champion Jack Dempsey. In a sort of semifinal for the world championship, the Wild bull of the *Pampas* fought the formidable American boxer Bill "KO" Brennan in New York on March 12, 1923. The Argentinean knocked his opponent around and finally sent him to the floor in the 12th round. On the crest of his own enthusiasm and that of the rest of the fans, Cristiani made *Fir-pobre-nan*. The title was a combination of the last two names played on the word "*pobre*," meaning "poor." "Pobre Brennan, pobre Brennan!," exclaimed Quirino 60 years later.

The match with Dempsey for the world title took place on the evening of September 14, 1923 at the Polo Ground in New York. About 80,000 people watched it, and contributed to the record proceeds of more than one million dollars (in 1923). "The gladiators only fought for three minutes and fifty-seven seconds, but during that brief time they engaged in the most savage title match in history," wrote journalist Paul Sann. "Both men emerged covered in blood and glory." Firpo threw Dempsey out of the ring with a violent right during the first round. American journalists on the sidelines hurried to push the battered champion through the ropes before the referee called a knock out. In the second round, Dempsey threw the winning punch and knocked his adversary out. Sann condemned the journalists' behavior as "unfair, unsportsmanlike and illegal," but everyone had to accept the final verdict. The Argentineans talked about it for weeks, and Quirino Cristiani made one of his most popular short films, titled *Firpo-Dempsey*. He never tired of saying, "Firpo had already won!" The match was one of the first great successes for another large-scale entertainment media: Radio. The newspaper *La Nación* sponsored the initiative that enabled the newly opened station "Radio Cultura" to broadcast the match live.

In 1924, Italy's crown prince, Umberto di Savoia, visited Argentina.* Umberto was only 20, and he was tall and handsome. A few affectionately romantic stories were being whispered about him and certain young ladies. One of these involved the daughter of the Argentinean ambassador to Rome, Beatriz Gagliardo. During a ball in the Italian capital, the prince had taken a ring from the girl, and when she asked him to give it back, he replied that he would return it, but only in her native country. According to popular newspapers, this "interest" was the real reason for his visit to Rio del Plata. However, regardless of Umberto's feelings for Miss Gagliardo, that visit was not strictly formal since Cristiani titled the film he made for the occasion *Humbertito de garufa* (Little Umberto Has Fun). This is how he summarized the plot:

> Umberto was travelling to South America, and since he had been told that Buenos Aires was a nice place where the people were pleasant and he could have fun, he decided to see the city. He was tall, but his father, Vittorio Emanuele,

---

* Umberto was born in Racconigi on September 15, 1904 and died on March 18, 1983 in Geneva, Switzerland. He was known as the *May King* because he ascended to the throne after his father Vittorio Emanuele III abdicated on May 9, 1946 but reigned for less than a month. On June 2 of the same year, the Italian people passed a referendum to find the republic. Umberto II spent the last decades of his life in Portugal.

was very short. When it came time for the prince to leave, the king had to get a ladder to hug and kiss his son. Then "little Umberto" went to Buenos Aires, saw the shows, danced the tango, fell in love with a gaucho's daughter... In short, I invented a lot of things to portray the prince as a dynamic young man just having fun. At the end of the movie, he met Beatriz Gagliardo and returned her ring. It lasted four or five minutes, about 80 meters of film.

Reportedly, Prince Umberto liked the film a lot. Moreover, when he sent his compliments to the director, he also asked if it were possible to purchase a copy. Sixty years later, Cristiani said that the conversation went something like this:

I said, "Oh no, Umberto, I'll give you a copy." He said, "Oh, very well then, thank you, but how can I repay you?" I said, "There is no need. I am honored for you to have it. I consider it an accomplishment." And he said, "When you come to Italy, remember that you will be my guest, at my home." What, at your home... "Yes," he said, "you know that I live at the Quirinale palace, and since your name is Quirino that means that you are a son of the Quirinale. That makes the Quirinale your home too..." That's what was said.

Uruguayos for ever was a short film based on the achievements of Uruguayan soccer players who won the gold medal and the Paris Olympics in 1924. Cristiani commented:

This was another fun film, but it was also patriotic for the Uruguayans. It was an enormous success in Montevideo. I had taken the film there, and I managed to show it at the Solis Theater, where a theatrical production on the same subject was running. The author and director of the comedy really liked my film and decided to show it after that during intermissions. It was a very flattering success, and I got 10% of the proceeds. It was shown throughout the summer season, that is, as long as the theater presentation ran.[*]

There is no way for us to know if Cristiani made other films for public entertainment during this time period. Some sources mention at least one title, *Argentinos en Sevilla*, but there are no details, and making assumptions is useless, so we will just have to wait for something concrete to emerge from future research.

A more important project was his collaboration with José Arce and Oscar Ivanisevich, two world famous surgeons. They wanted Cristiani to make films that illustrated their technique. When he heard that they wanted him to watch the operations in order to understand just exactly what he would have had to draw and animate, he answered apprehensively that he would—if they agreed to have something strong to drink on hand.

Once the initial anxiety passed, Cristiani arranged a suitable perch over the operating table from where he could watch the surgeons' hands and record their gestures with his pencil and paper. He made two films, *Gastrotomía* and *Rinoplastía*, acclaimed for their precision and realism. Dr. Arce presented them at the medical congress in Seville in 1925, and they were well received. Later, Arce took the films to Paris, and there the works were purchased by the University of Sorbonne for educational purposes. *Le Journal* published the following comment: "We watched a film that is a novelty in the field of cinema, a significant technical work by a young Argentinean artist."

Another informational film deserves to be mentioned. It was commissioned by a building company, which improved the

---

[*] According to Cristiani's first reconstruction, the film illustrated Uruguay's victory at the Amsterdam Olympics. However, those games took place in 1928, and he was doing something else—as we will see in the next chapters. When I pointed this out to him, he wrote me a letter in which he dated the film to match the Paris Olympics of 1924, where Uruguay had also won the title, and remembering that he had made it before making the medical films in 1925.

Madero Harbor of Buenos Aires after winning the bid from the Ministry of Public Works.

All the work was visible, from the beginning: how they took the land from the river, then the construction, everything. Until the total construction of the harbor was visible, including the recreational businesses on the beach. I never heard anything more about it, as it was done on commission. They paid me, and that was it.

REFERENCES

Cristiani, Q. (1917). *El Apóstol.*
Cristiani, Q. (1919). *Los que ligan.*
Cristiani, Q. (1923). *Fir-pobre-nan.*
Cristiani, Q. (1923). *Firpo-Dempsey.*
Cristiani, Q. (1924). *Humbertito de garufa.*
Cristiani, Q. (1924). *Uruguayos for ever.*
Cristiani, Q. (1925). *Gastrotomía.*
Cristiani, Q. (1925). *Rinoplastía.*
Cristiani, Q. (2008). *The mystery of the first animated movies.*

CHAPTER 12

Cristiani in Advertising

D URING THIS TIME, CRISTIANI was busy drawing, animating, and directing—and producing. He had a tiny studio in *calle* Lavalle and he worked primarily with advertising.

He recalled:

> I contacted the owner of a cloth factory who loved the cinema. The idea was to offer to show free films to the public on the street, with a "movie-truck" that would show short films with animated advertising as interludes. He was to finance the project. We needed to buy an old truck that was still in good shape, and then fix it up nice and pretty. To start with, we decided to do a three-minute animated drawing with an advertising message, and then present it to a few possible clients to see if they were interested. At that time, there were two large match factories: La Compañia general de Fósforos (the most important) that made wood and wax matches, and the Fábrica Mantero (paper matches). So I made Las aventuras de Fosforito (The Adventures of the Match Man).

There was a box of matches. Two came out, with the faces of a man and a woman. Then they were shown with human clothes and a human figure. I drew them in a forest where it was kind of dark, like two sweethearts. He said to her, "Fosforita, my heart burns when you're around!" And she said, "Make sure your head doesn't catch on fire!" Then they hugged and kissed and when the two match heads rubbed together, they caught fire and the forest lit up with a bright light. Then the flame went out and the figures regained their original match-like form and went back into the box. This was in the foreground, and the name Fiammiferi Victoria was visible. The speaker (this was during the time of silent films) then said, "They give off more light and last longer!" However, I must tell you that paper matches didn't last long at all. Only long enough to light a cigarette.

The results were excellent. They bought the truck, overhauled it, and made it into a luxury mobile cinema equipped with a projector, accumulators, and a dismountable screen. The films were back projected: the projector was behind the screen instead of behind the audience. It was fixed to the truck to avoid the headache of moving it and setting it up each time. The driver and his helper were responsible for the show, so one ran the projector, whereas the other entertained the audience.

We showed short films, like Charlie Chaplin's first works or those of other comedians who were out of the market but were a surprise for new generations. These older films "slept" in their distributors' warehouses, and I rented them for very little. We alternated these films with our short film-advertisements, which the public really liked. We showed them in town squares and open spaces, and at the end, we used a megaphone to tell the audience when and where the next showing would be held.

The initiative was called Publi-Cinema and, according to Cristiani, it was Argentina's first encounter with film advertising, which would come to theaters at a later time.

Everything went fine until the inevitable happened. They managed to attract so many people that the city government prohibited the showings because they "disturbed public order and interfered with traffic." In fact, the crowd would often ignore traffic and stand calmly in the middle of the road.

> We made many, many films for lots and lots of products. I remember one for *yerba mate* Cruz del Sur.* We protrayed Flammarion, the astronomer, with rhyming subtitles: "El gran sabio Flammarion/descubre con gran contento/en el azul firmamento/una gran constelación." Then there was a star that moved to the center of the screen and turned into a package of *mate*: Yerba Mate Cruz del Sur. The Southern Cross is the most important constellation of the southern hemisphere and therefore also of the Argentineans.

The prohibition of street advertising, *callejera*, did not discourage Cristiani. He decided to take his idea inside.

> We tried with a downtown theater. At that time, theaters would turn on the lights during intermission and they would lower a curtain in front of the screen with ugly advertisements stuck on it. I convinced the owner to change this practice and instead project animated advertisements in semi-darkness. Patrons liked this system. Our first film of this kind was *La camisa del hombre feliz*.

This initiative worked well until the end of the 1930s when a competitor emerged, Emelco, owned by brothers Kurt and Frederick Lowe.

---

* *Yerba mate* is a bush. Its leaves are used to make a tea that is very popular in southern-most South America.

In the end, Cristiani gave up the fight against advertising done with human actors, but not before he made a fair amount of money.

Cristiani was also interested in another area, and it was almost a real job: Inventions.

> When I decided to go into business for myself, I invented a filming system that allowed me to work alone, without those people that the Valle studios used to pompously call "lights technicians" and "operators." I had a filming worktable built, with a camera mounted on it with the lens angled downward—that is—toward the tabletop where I arranged drawings and figurines. It was all mechanized. The camera, modified so that it shot one frame at a time, was run with a button that I pushed with my right foot, while with the left foot I pushed the button that turned the lights on and off. That way my hands were free to do the animation of the drawings and figurines.

His inventions were not confined to the field of cinema: there was also a coffee maker that heated coffee and milk simultaneously (in two separate compartments) and a matchbox with a no-spill opening.

REFERENCE

Tolstói, L. (1828–1910). *La camisa del hombre feliz.*

CHAPTER **13**

The Most Ambitious Project of the Estudios Cristiani

I N 1927 QUIRINO CRISTIANI was named art director of Metro–Goldwyn–Mayer's advertizing service in Argentina. His job was to create posters that would be placed on the streets to announce the arrival of a new movie from Hollywood's largest producer.

In his old age, Cristiani fondly recalled his posters for Greta Garbo's films and for *The Love Parade* by Ernst Lubitsch, with Maurice Chevalier and Jeanette MacDonald.

This new volume of work made it impossible to continue contributing to publications (*El Magazine, Última Hora, Caricatura Universal, Humorismo Porteño, Media Noche*) to which he had continued to send drawings and vignettes. Therefore, Cristiani's journalistic career ended.

During that time, he had left his studio in calle Lavalle and had set up a studio in the back yard of his home in Avenida Cabildo 1518. Later, he had to rent another apartment to have enough space for himself, his brushes, and the machinery. At last, in 1928, he opened the Estudios Cristiani, in calle Sarmiento 2121. The head of MGM in Argentina, Mr. Feidelbaum, was accommodating with respect to his art director's second job, and entrusted him with the task of using his equipment for animated films to prepare Spanish subtitles for the imported American films. This collaboration between the Estudios Cristiani and MGM turned out to be essential over the following years.

However, political events were in the making, and would soon capture Cristiani's attention.

In 1922, Yrigoyen was forbidden by the constitution to run for the presidency again, and he yielded to another radical, moderate Marcelo T. de Alvear. The party had split into the *personalistas* (Yrigoyenists) and the *antipersonalistas* (moderates and those who did not like the omnipotent persona of the leader).* In 1928, Yrigoyen could once again run for office (two terms were allowed as long as they were not consecutive), was elected, but his second term created more problems than his first. Quirino Cristiani once again felt the desire to target the president with his humor. Using the tried and true method of the cut-out, sewn-together figurines, he and a small team started work on a new project—and this time he also had efficient machinery. The work was based on a subject written by Eduardo González Lanuza titled *Peludópolis,* that is: "The city of the Peludo" (Peludo was Yrigoyen's nickname) (Figures 13.1 and 13.2).

Cristiani did everything himself for this third feature. He created and designed the characters, and did the animation, directing, and production. He had several helpers (some sources exaggerate with stories about "an army" of collaborators), but he was not obliged to accept any suggestions about the creative aspect. Or rather, suggestions were made, but they arose out of circumstances. He started in 1929 with a certain approach and a particular subject, and the movie had to be altered due to events.

---

* See Appendix 1.

FIGURE 13.1 President Hipólito Yrigoyen with a political follower.

FIGURE 13.2 Another caricature of Hipólito Yrigoyen, explaining his nickname "El peludo" (The armadillo).

In fact, the Peludo did not stay in the Casa Rosada long enough to allow the satirical film to be completed and be its legitimate target. On September 6, 1930 the *revolución* led by General José Félix Uriburu removed him from office (Figures 13.3a, b and 13.4).

(a)

(b)

FIGURE 13.3 (a,b) Quirino Cristiani during the making of *Peludópolis*. Several sewn-together cut-out figures are visible, shown on different shelves next to the animator and under the filming table. The vertical camera can be seen over the table, and the lighting system is set up on the sides.

FIGURE 13.4   The figurine of Yrigoyen used for *Peludópolis,* showing its size as compared to a person's hand.

REFERENCES

Cristiani, Q. (1931). *Peludópolis.*
Lubitsch, E. (1929). *The love parade.*

CHAPTER 14

Peludópolis: The First Animated Feature Length Film with Sound

The Government ship sails across the Ocean waves, surrounded by sharks. A few modern pirates, led by an extraordinary character, "El Peludo," attack the ship and drive away its captain, "El Pelado." Now in command of the ship, the pirates continue sailing until they reach a tasty island, the "República Quesolandina" (the Republic of Cheeseland).* They settle here, and have hilarious adventures, until a paper boat appears on the horizon. Its captain is the "General Provisional," who along with "Juan Pueblo," begins to work on repairing things, with the ultimate goal of restoring order to the unbalanced island.

---

* Cristiani called it *Quesolandina* to rhyme with *Argentina*.

This is a summary of *Peludópolis*, written by Quirino Cristiani in 1931 when he was preparing to present the film to the public. Originally, the satirical movie was supposed to highlight the inefficiency and greed of Yrigoyen's ministers, who had become the laughing stock of Buenos Aires. He purposely named the pirates' island Quesolandina because in Rio de la Plata, saying that a politician "liked cheese" meant that he was doing his own thing with public money.

The captain of the government ship was El Pelado, President Alvear (the nickname refers to his baldness). It appears that Cristiani adopted a vaguely *antipersonalista* approach: although Alvear had never directly joined the more conservative faction of the radicalists, his personality and ideology actually made him part of it. Alvear is not however portrayed in a flattering manner. He is shown lying lazily on a chaise longue in a bathing suit with a disinterested look and wearing a top hat (radicals from rich families wore that hat called in Spanish *galerita*). The anti-Yrigoyenists were not given a positive image either: the later Uriburu's minister of the interior, Matias Sánchez Sorondo, was portrayed as proud and unreliable, and General Justo bore the nickname Paracaidista, (which literally means "parachutist" but carries another connotation meaning "social climber" or "opportunist") (Figures 14.1 through 14.5).

The events of September 1930 created unpredicted problems. The film was three-fourths finished, and now it was no longer current. All of the irony aimed at the radical government had lost its meaning, since the radical government no longer existed.

Cristiani began redoing the movie. Lots of work had to be thrown away, and a new ending had to be invented, which showed that Pepe Provisional (General Uriburu, of course) arrives to fix things, and the newly fashioned character Juan Pueblo helps him. "Juan Pueblo" is the proverbial personification of the average Argentine, in the same way that "John Bull" symbolizes England or the average Englishman, and "John Q. Public" represents the average American. Therefore, the film depicted the Argentinean people,

FIGURE 14.1 Cover of the advertisement flyer for *Peludópolis*. Top: heads of Yrigoyen, Elpidio González, and Uriburu. Bottom: Yrigoyen on the island Quesolandina in front of his crew. Dressed as a priest is José Luis Cantilo, a fervent Catholic who was among the founders of the Union Cívica Radical party and also held several positions, including his appointment in 1917 as an interventor of the province of Buenos Aires (replacing Governor Marcelino Ugarte).

FIGURE 14.2 Cover of the advertisement flyer for *Peludópolis*. On his beach chair, Marcelo T. de Alvear.

(a)

(b)

FIGURE 14.3 (a,b) Advertisement flyer for *Peludópolis*. Clockwise, starting from the top left: El Peludo INRIgoyen (the joke targeted Yrigoyen for being "deified"); Agustín P. Justo; Elpidio González

(*Continued*)

FIGURE 14.4 Advertisement flyer for *Peludópolis*. The temporary president, José Félix Uriburu (mustachioed) and his family at the premiere of the film.

FIGURE 14.3 (Continued) (known as "de Córdoba" because he went to school there); Pepe Provisional (the temporary president José Félix Uriburu); two unidentified characters; ministers and other characters from the Destino clan (exponents of the paramilitary teams of the Unión Cívica Radical party, nicknamed the "clan radical"). The second-in-command Tamborcito (José P. Tamburini, minister in Alvear's government). El Pelado Baibiene (Marcelo T. de Alvear; the word "baibiene," pronounced "vaiviene," – "goes forth and back" – suggests that he sways easily); Calafate Per'es el Colmo (Enrique Pérez Celmán, minister in Yrigoyen's government, "per'es el colmo" is the deformation of "pero es el colmo" = "but this is the last straw"); O.K. Rina Horacio Uñanarte (Horacio B. Oyhanarte, Yrigoyen's Minister of Foreign Affairs; O.K. Rina is pronounced "ocarina," Uñanarte indicates the character's greedy nature, as uña = claw), and the boatswain Sancho Orondo (Matías Sánchez Sorondo, Uriburu's Minister of the Interior).

FIGURE 14.5   Advertisement flyer for *Peludópolis*. Nonliteral translation of the little poem: "Impartial viewer, in this show you will find neither political party propaganda nor insults to anyone. It is happy and funny, and if it teases the Doctor, it does so without hate nor spite. Do not watch it with suspicion; making fun of the Peludo is almost like doing him a favour." In the upper drawing, Juan Pueblo states a point to generals Justo and Uriburu. In the lower drawing, Juan Pueblo, relaxed, can enjoy his guitar.

together with a military "fixer-upper" able to restore their own country. It was an optimistic, wishful thinking ending.

Peludópolis was shown as a "premiere" on September 16, 1931 (or possibly, September 18) at the Cine Renacimiento. It lasted one hour and twenty minutes, and the temporary president himself, José Félix Uriburu, was in the audience. At the end of the film, he congratulated Cristiani and defined the film as a "great work of satire and a noteworthy acclamation of the Argentinean armed forces."

Actually, Cristiani had mixed feelings. On one hand, he did not know what to make of Yrigoyen, Uriburu, and Justo: the situation was too confusing. On the other, he did not know how to present himself to the public, who was just as confused as he was. In his opening credits, he inserted a short poem as a sort of disclaimer against passionate reactions that different factions might have had on seeing the film:

Espectador imparcial:
No hallarás en esta vista
Ni prédica partidista
Ni insultos a tal o cual.
Es alegre, espiritual,
Y si lo cacha al Dotor
Es sin odios ni rencor.
No la mires con recelo,
Tomarle al Peludo el pelo
Es casi hacerle un favor.*

If the events of 1930 had created big problems during the production phase, the events of 1931 created worse problems during the phase of presenting the film to viewers. It seemed impossible that Juan Pueblo might gain advantages from Pepe Provisional, or that he could roll up his sleeves and work together with the politician to fix the republic of Quesolandina—or better, Argentina.

A few months after the film's premiere, a new president came to live in the Casa Rosada. General Agustín P. Justo was a smart politician, but without the platform and charisma that could spark hope in the population. People had started to vote for the radical party again and, though the more famous Yrigoyenists were all either behind bars or in exile, the Peludo was regaining popularity with his voters. His home had been broken into by vandals and thieves during the unrest following the takeover, but demonstrators had been shocked and shamed by the incident. His furnishings were poor and he had few personal possessions, signs of an

---

* Nonliteral translation: Impartial viewer, in this show you will find neither political party propaganda nor insults to anyone. It is happy and funny, and if it teases the Doctor, it does so without hate or spite. Do not watch it with suspicion; making fun of the Peludo is almost like doing him a favor.

honest and frugal lifestyle. This is why *Peludópolis* was unsuccessful with the public. It was a half success for the press, judging from the reviews that have been preserved, and that are printed in Figure 14.6a–c (with one general comment: that reviewers at that time did not appear to be very knowledgeable or have clear ideas about animated films).

The daily newspaper *La Nación* commented:

> "The film can be considered as one of the greatest efforts of national cinema. […] The work was extremely complex, and we must admit that Cristiani has come out a winner. For over an hour, the caricatures of Peludópolis amuse viewers and keep them laughing at allusions to people and events that everyone is talking about. […] The public applauds each character as it appears, all accompanied by music and funny captions. Their behavior is coherent with well-known events that occurred during the last regime. However, there is no doubt that the film would have been more effective if it had followed a more direct approach, and if the figurines (which were rather solemn) had moved more. In this film, the artist Cristiani shows singular talent for the difficult genre of animated drawings."

Prensa issued the following comment:

> "Cristiani, the famous artist, […] demonstrates that he has the ability to produce a harmonious, funny film. His aim is simple and wholesome; the movie humbly succeeds in conveying his message. He manages his pencil with lively talent in the field of political satire. Also, he humorously conveys amusing aspects of the institutional life of our country that have occurred during the past two years. The different lines of his pencil overcome the inherent difficulties of the complex procedure of animated drawing. Cristiani draws caricatures of men who were in the public eye and others that are now well known in national politics. Viewers enjoy his

(a)

(b)

FIGURE 14.6 (a–c) Advertisement flyer for *Peludópolis*. Clippings about the film. (*Continued*)

(c)

FIGURE 14.6 (Continued) (a–c) Advertisement flyer for *Peludópolis*. Clippings about the film.

funny creations, many of which are simply brilliant. What else could we want? In this simple film, without being presumptuous, Cristiani gives us a commendable work of political satire with the animated drawings of *Peludópolis*."

"The popular and acclaimed artist, Quirino Cristiani, is Argentina's own expert in animated drawings," wrote *El Diario*, "Now he gives us greater evidence of his talent, and an abundant dose of his creativity with the film *Peludópolis*, that [...] was shown three times a day at the cinema Renacimiento. It is a caricature film with sound, with talking and singing. This is the first time that something of this type has been done in our country. [...] But the film's essential quality is the brilliance of its creator, who develops a comical-satirical theme about current political events. [...] Our most famous politicians grace the screen as well-drawn caricatures, with recognizable physiognomy and character (authentic or attributed by public opinion). The type of ridicule that they are targeted with is along the lines of what is usually printed in the newspapers, no more. It is not angry satire, nor is it a zealous amplification of current events. This is how Cristiani agrees with the spirit of the general public, and he is rewarded with their applause. Viewers will find many humorous moments in this film: in the caricatures themselves and the funny captions, the songs and the many comical details of the film."

Noticias Gráficas commented:

"*Peludópolis* [...] pokes fun at recent political events that occurred in Argentina during the past two years. It is all the interpretation of an intelligent artist. Which is to say that his impressions reduce to mathematical lines and situations. [...] The passage from one drawing to the next has the same fluidity as the animated vignettes by American artists, and the music by Vázquez Vigo accompanies each hilarious scene of the film with great vivacity. What more could we want? Cristiani has made the first feature length film with animated drawings, for our country, [*sic*] and what's more, he gave that film the particular feel of a *cachada porteña*."[*]

"There is no doubt that the artist Cristiani's work constitutes one of the greatest efforts in our nation's film history," commented *La Razón*, "if we consider the difficulties associated with films of this type. Especially here in our country, where technical equipment has not been perfected until recently. Without great ambitions, simply and very ingeniously, the author has completed a harmonious, funny and light-hearted work of satire about men and events of the regime overturned

---

[*] This term can be translated approximately as "humor as the Buenos Aires inhabitants understand it."

by the *coup d'etat*. If the theme had been developed more directly, the film would have been more effective. Nevertheless, the public had no trouble understanding it, and laughed heartily at each of the well-known characters as they made their appearance. *Peludópolis* absolutely keeps its promises."

Última Hora added more detail:

"The prologue to this film consists of scenes filmed in the studio of the preparation of character figurines. Viewers really liked this, since the procedure has been almost a secret up until now. [...] Undeniably, *Peludópolis* has many merits, and the first is the technical procedure used to create it and bring it to the screen. The second consists in the fact that Cristiani has drawn each character with the physical appearance that makes him identifiable. The public enjoyed the film, and came out of the theater very pleased."

And *El Mundo* said:

"Cristiani wanted to score a point for himself by completing this extraordinary effort which is the film *Peludópolis*, a work of political satire in animated drawings. And the truth is that his effort is almost excessive, so much so that he almost scored two points instead of one...especially if we consider the level of difficulty that he had to overcome, in this area which is always poor in elements and materials for work of this nature. However, even when the film shows an authentic surplus of ingenuity and lightness, with several ideas that are all perfectly humorous, the truth is that concentrating too much on one idea frequently causes slip-ups. Some lines were not really that well aimed, and some episodes were conceived and made imperfectly. The music is easy and very appropriate, and contributes to the success of *Peludópolis* which, we must say, is funny and was appreciated by viewers."

Another work of documentarist Gabriele Zucchelli's finds was a six-minute "making of" showing the creation of *Peludópolis*. With the title *Una visita a los Estudios Cristiani*, this promotional documentary was shown before the feature started, to highlight the fact that the feature represented a novelty for filmgoers at that time, since both animation and "talking movies" were quite rare. The brief film shows a very active studio with some assistants and several specialized technicians busy working on various steps of the animation process. The documentary contains an excerpted scene of El Peludo dancing a tango with a girl, and also the technical production steps: puppets being cut-out, film being shot and developed, and finally the registration of music with José Vázquez Vigo directing the orchestra. Animation techniques are illustrated by Quirino Cristiani himself, who was 34 at the time. It is worth noting that the cut-outs did not move similar to articulated figurines, but in phases—as in proper drawn animation.

When Hipólito Yrigoyen died on July 3, 1933, the population responded with a colossal, solemn tribute. Quirino Cristiani was among those that walked in the funeral procession behind the casket, which pall bearers carried on their shoulders along *Avenida* Callao. In his words, it was an "impressive and quiet multitude" ("impresionante y silenciosa multitud"). "Por ética, y en su memoria" (for reasons of ethics and in his memory), in addition to the concrete market-related reasons, Cristiani recalled all copies of *Peludópolis* that were still in circulation and put them in storage. Financially, the project ended with a loss of about 25,000 pesos. One important event had happened, though, which had pleased him immensely: His father had been present the night of the premier at the Cine Renacimiento. Luigi Cristiani, 70 years old and resigned to the fact that his youngest son had become a *pintamonos* instead of a doctor, had watched bursting with pride while Quirino received the compliments of the President of the Republic. And in that victorious moment, neither of them cared about political opinions.

REFERENCE

Cristiani, Q. (1931). *Peludópolis*.

CHAPTER 15

Cristiani as an Entrepreneur

I N ARGENTINA, SOUND FILMS arrived on June 19, 1929. The era began at the cinema Grand Splendid with the film *The Divine Lady*. It was directed by Frank Lloyd (who was awarded an Oscar for it) and starring Corinne Griffith and Victor Varconi, which narrated the love story between Lady Hamilton and British Admiral Horatio Nelson.

In spite of the abyss separating American film technology from that of Argentinean films, Rio de la Plata people really worked hard to keep pace with the times. The country's most famous director, José Agustín Ferreyra, was asked to return home from Spain, where he was living temporarily. Federico Valle saw to it personally. *La canción del gaucho* (1930) and *Muñequitas porteñas* (1931) were the first sound films of the national industry, and they marked the second phase of Ferreyra's career.

Quirino Cristiani, who also came to the big screen with his big production in 1931, was prepared for action in a way that no other animator in the world was, both in the absolute sense of the word and regarding the national film industry. Only Walt Disney had been able to present an animated film with sound (*Steamboat Willie*, 1928) at such a short time after the first live-action film with talking and sound (*The Jazz Singer*, 1927). Furthermore, *Steamboat Willie* was a short film and, if we consider the technical and economical conditions, the two films are incomparable. Cristiani had used discs to endow his films with sound, in line with the Vitaphone system that was pioneered in Argentina by Francisco Chiavarra and Alfredo Murúa from SIDE (Sociedad impresora de discos electrofónicos). A sound track on the optical track would come later. In the field of Argentinean animation, Cristiani would be the first again with the film *Mono Relojero*, which we will examine later.

In the meantime, during the year that *Peludópolis* came out, 1931, Cristiani transferred his film laboratory from calle Sarmiento 2121 to calle José Evaristo Uriburu 460. This was the beginning of the development phase of his industrial work.

When the laboratory opened in 1928, it was first designed for the purpose of making Cristiani's films (for advertising and other purposes). Then, the local Metro–Goldwyn–Mayer office had started commissioning work and the range of activities widened gradually. The problem that distributors of foreign films most often faced was the substitution of damaged parts of the copies. The beginning and end of the reels were the areas that were most likely to be damaged. The most effective solution was to find a copy in perfect condition, make an internegative of the damaged footage, and then reprint it. Cristiani's laboratory handled this type of work during its early years. Then the laboratory started to produce whole reels, and from 1931 onward, the laboratory handled a whole range of diverse activities.

There were several laboratories at that time in addition to Cristiani's: Alex, Decker, Tecnofilm, and Biasotti. Alex was the most successful; it was founded in 1928 (the same year as Cristiani) by Alejandro "Alex" Connio and his son Carlos Connio Santini. The level of equipment and service was not internationally competitive at any of these places. It was impossible to maintain a uniform level of production in printing, and therefore every film stock had its own level of photographic quality. As a result, a feature film would have continuous deformities. Films were mounted by hand, with technicians merely scrutinizing the film without the use of special equipment to try to recognize the scenes (only the better equipped had magnifying glasses). The first editing machine was imported in 1937; the first optical printer in 1939. The Alex Company was responsible for promoting this modern technology: Carlos Connio Santini spent four months in 1936 studying at Eastman Kodak in Rochester, United States, and afterward was able to advance on the market against his competitors. Until the end of the century, Alex was a giant in the Argentinean film industry.

Cristiani did not have the same mentality as Carlos Connio Santini. Although Santini was essentially a technician who happened to deal in filmmaking with entrepreneurial flair, Cristiani worked on a vast array of activities. His studio worked mainly with foreign companies. Metro, Fox, United Artists, and Columbia sent him lavender* copies of their films, and the laboratory produced the internegatives that were then used to produce several copies of each film for the local distribution offices of each company. But a second task gradually developed into an important job: translating the dialogs and inserting them as subtitles on the copies themselves. This was the true specialty of Cristiani's company, and they were very proud of it for many years.

---

* The *lavender* copy (sometimes spelled *lavander*) was a *spare positive countertype*, in other words, a positive film derived from the original negative, but printed on a low contrast medium. It was possible to obtain a new negative of fairly good quality from the *lavender*, whereas a normal positive would have produced a countertype without shades of gray (lavender copies were only used for black and white films). The name derives from the color of the aforementioned low contrast material.

In addition to this, there was distribution. Cristiani remembered the films he distributed with a mixture of pleasure and regret. There were some German films during the 1930s that he recalled as being artistically noteworthy but not well-liked by the public ("Eran películas muy finas, pero comercialmente... nada!"). He particularly remembered *Marta* (which could be *Martha*, or *Letzte Rose* by Karl Anton, 1936) and *Peer Gynt* (most probably the film by Fritz Wendhausen, 1934). He also distributed Italian films with opera singer Beniamino Gigli. He worked on the newsreels, called *noticieros*. Cristiani reached his zenith in this particular field during the period from December 3, 1933 to December 26, 1933, when he went to Uruguay to film the VII International Conference of the American States that was taking place in Montevideo. The event was held at the Palacio Legislativo, with delegates from all of the South American countries and the U.S. Secretary of State Cordell Hull. Cristiani (always sensitive to presidents) was highly praised by Uruguay's president Gabriel Terra, and invited by him to the grand gala banquet, which was held in a place that the artist fondly remembered as "de privilegio."

The Laboratorios Cristiani was destined to remain in business until 1961, when the competition and damage from fires forced them to sell. But up to that date, they built a substantial part of the history of Argentina's film industry. For years, they ranked among the leaders of the nation. In 1941, they bought more advanced machinery, which neutralized their rival Alex's advantage: automatic printers, synchronization benches, sensitometry equipment, and editing machines.*

In addition to all this, Cristiani also worked diligently in advertising. Finally, he tried to teach animation technique in a correspondence course (Figure 15.1).

---

* The company was restructured, with Quirino and his son Atilio as limited partners, and Francesco Cristiani (Quirino's brother) and Luis Quirino Cristiani (Cristiani's other son) as general partners.

He believed that he would, as usual, carry out this project enthusiastically while looking ahead to the future, in collaboration with the Escuelas Técnicas. The schools did not participate for long, though, and he found that no one was willing to put forth the capital to finance the idea, so he had to quit. "Only a few enthusiastic kids came to the first lessons," he said. "I refunded the money that they had paid in advance. But, I was able to attract the attention of some of them by allowing them to remain in the studio while I was making films. This is how I met Quinterno, Oliva, Kayser, Sara Cetrán..."

(a)

FIGURE 15.1 (a–c) Poster of the correspondence school of animation designed by Cristiani. The captions praise the easy method and say that the cels are purchased directly in the United States. *(Continued)*

(b)

FIGURE 15.1 (Continued) (a–c) Poster of the correspondence school of animation designed by Cristiani. The captions praise the easy method and say that the cels are purchased directly in the United States.

(*Continued*)

(c)

FIGURE 15.1 (Continued)   (a–c) Poster of the correspondence school of animation designed by Cristiani. The captions praise the easy method and say that the cels are purchased directly in the United States.

It is not clear if Cristiani also made a film of his own, in addition to advertising materials, between the years 1931 and 1938. But it is certain that the last important chapter of this business of his own started this year, 1938, due to a meeting with Constancio C. Vigil.

REFERENCES

Anton, K. (1936). *Martha.*

Anton, K. (1936). *Peer Gynt.*

Cristiani, Q. (1931). *Peludópolis.*

Cristiani, Q. (1938). *Mono Relojero.*

Crosland, A. (1927). *The Jazz Singer.*

Ferreyra, J. A. (1930). *La canción del gaucho.*

Ferreyra, J. A. (1930). *Muñequitas porteñas.*

Lloyd, F. (1929). *The Divine Lady.*

Piette, C. and U. Iwerks. (1928). *Steamboat Willie.*

Wendhausen, F. (1934). *Peer Gynt.*

CHAPTER 16

Constancio C. Vigil and the Story of *El mono relojero*

In the modern world, cinema is the best form of communication for spreading ideas, and therefore it is important that it be used for educational purposes. [...] Ancient apologues and ancient fables, which were used to impart moral instruction to many generations, and also to entertain them, still have the same impact today, though in a latent form. However, it is necessary to give them a new format, so that they will take on that immediacy which is imperceptible in the now antiquated format of literary expression. The only way to bring out this complex of emotions and examples, which humanity has always needed, is this: bring it to the big screen, translated into living language and direct communication through animated drawings. [...] My support for Quirino Cristiani for turning my story *El mono relojero* into a film shows my firm desire to open a productive channel of teachings and healthy fun for our people (Figure 16.1).

FIGURE 16.1   Constancio C. Vigil, author of the story *El mono relojero*, producer of the film, publisher.

These comments, released in 1938 to the magazine *Cine argentino*, could be considered the authorization of Constancio C. Vigil for the film that Quirino Cristiani made based on his children's story.

Vigil was a political thinker, writer, journalist, and an editor. In particular, he was a narrator and thinker in the area of education.

"Todo un señor personaje," was how Cristiani defined him.

Vigil was born in 1876 in Uruguay, in the *departamento* of Rocha. His interest in literature emerged during childhood, and in time he wrote poems, prose, and essays about different subjects. He edited and directed magazines and periodicals; he fought political battles in favor of the inter-American brotherhood and a future of peace. His story *El Erial* (1915) made him very popular and was respected throughout the Spanish-speaking American countries. This book, with its strong moral theme, was translated into several different languages. It came out in English with the title *The Fallow Land* (Vigil 1945).

In Buenos Aires, where Vigil moved at the beginning of the century, he founded the Editorial Atlántida.

His company quickly became very successful, and he went on to build a publishing empire. He published different types of magazines and book, often with large circulations, such as the sporting magazine *El Gráfico* and the children's publication *Billiken*, both introduced in 1919 and still on the newsstands. Under the leadership of his son, Carlos Vigil, the company continued being one of the strongest publishing houses in the country, until the retirement of the founding family in 2000 and the sale to Mexico's Televisa in 2007.

Constancio Vigil never abandoned his political–civil activity, and for that reason he was nominated for the Nobel Peace Prize because of his mediation work to end the Chaco War (1929–1935) between Bolivia and Paraguay. Nevertheless, his stories for children were responsible for his popularity with the general public. His best known work was the story of the "Watchmaker Monkey" (in Spanish *El mono relojero*), and these were stories, not fables. Despite the fact that its characters were talking animals instead of people, *El mono relojero* does not have much in common with Aesop or Phaedrus. The style is deliberately not quaint, and fluid but cutting. Its theme centers around ethics, which create a world where duty is the key and few concessions for pleasure are allowed.

The plot begins with a watchmaker's shop where there is a monkey on a chain, which attracts the attention of passersby and customers. The monkey wants to be free, and escapes after a few scenes showing his various antics in the shop. He hides in the forest, but he does not know how to adapt to the environment and his rifle (a reference to human civilization) is useless, mainly because it is only a toy. So, the monkey decides to open a business. He goes back to the watchmaker's shop one night, steals a few watches, and returns to the forest where he tries to sell them to the animals—which should be a very good target group for his business because none of them own a watch. His commercial attempt ends in humiliating misunderstandings, and he is lucky to escape with his life. His only option is to go back to the watchmaker's shop. His owner is not hostile, but this time he sets some conditions: The monkey is required to work if he wants to eat, and that means he must clean the shop and the window every day. The monkey agrees, but only for a while. After a bit of manual labor, the monkey runs away again. The first leg of his new journey takes place in a school, where he entertains the children and learns that if he buries seeds he will gather fruits later on. Stupidly, the monkey becomes convinced that any object will sprout like a seed if it is buried, so he collects a sack full of buttons, erasers, and pens and goes out in search of a field to cultivate. He finds one that he likes near a swamp, but there is a mean stork who wants to take advantage of the monkey's work for his own purpose. The monkey realizes that the bird is too arrogant, and he escapes before the harvest season. In the final part of his adventures, the monkey finds himself chained to a traveling organ grinder begging for money. One day he meets the watchmaker, who recognizes him and makes fun of him.

When Vigil contacted Cristiani, he proposed a more ambitious project than just making a simple short film. His initial idea was to make a movie version of each of his stories, so after *El mono relojero* the next film would have been *La hormiguita viajera* ("The Traveling Ant") and then *La familia Conejola* ("The Rabbit Family") and so on. However, the first film ended up being the last as well. We do not know why: Cristiani said it was because the writer passed away, but this is unlikely. Vigil died 16 years later, in 1954. Whatever reasons there may have been did not interfere with the relationship between Cristiani and Vigil, which always remained in good standing.

For the first time, since working with Valle and Della Valle y Fauvety, Quirino Cristiani was not producing his own work. Vigil paid him 15,000 pesos for the movie, and Cristiani directed it and provided personnel and equipment. Circumstances did create momentary friction at times, but the film is incomparably precious in retrospect. *El mono relojero* is in fact the only film of Cristiani's that has survived, because it was kept in the producer's archives and not in the director's. Therefore, it did not burn.

REFERENCES

Cristiani, Q. (1938). *El mono relojero.*
Vigil, C. C. (1915). *El Erial.*
Vigil, C. C. (1927). *La hormiguita viajera.*
Vigil, C. C. (1943). *La familia Conejola.*
Vigil, C. C. (1945). *The Fallow Land,* edited by L. Smith. Harper & Brothers, New York.

CHAPTER 17

El mono relojero
on the Screen

S EVERAL PEOPLE TOOK PART in this film. More than a normal short film would require and more, perhaps, than would really have been required. The story was adapted by Eleazar P. Maestre, and Federico Ribas created the characters. Ribas was a Spanish artist who had just come to the New World after enduring the tragedy of the Civil War that started in his country in 1936. The backgrounds were painted by Eglantina Villagra, with the collaboration of Rosarivo and Kras. Animation was directed by Juan Oliva and Kayser, filming was entrusted to 24-year-old Luis Quirino Cristiani, and the music and sound were managed by José Vázquez Vigo (who had done the same work for *Peludópolis*). Finally, the voices were created by Pepe Iglesias, better known as "El Zorro," an impressionist and comedian who worked in radio and later on in movies (Figures 17.1 and 17.2a–c).

FIGURE 17.1 Working at the *Mono relojero*. From left: Kayser (Bogoslav Petanjek), unknown: 24-year-old Luís Quirino Cristiani. Sitting: Quirino Cristiani.

From a technical standpoint, the film was done with the most modern methods. It was the first Argentinean animated film with an optical sound track (disks were now considered prehistoric), and the animation was done on cel, the technique normally used by American filmmakers. This film was not in color, but here we need to remember that color was a novelty even in the United States and an experiment in Europe: There was nothing strange about there being no other option in a cinematically gregarious country like Argentina.

Original photographs show that the Cristiani studio was very well equipped. The vertical camera, sound, and mounting equipment, and inbetweening and coloring room were all the epitome of order and efficiency.

Advertising films had made it necessary to adopt the use of cel for animation. Cristiani reluctantly abandoned his own original

(a)

FIGURE 17.2   (a–c) A press report on the making of *El mono relojero*.
(*Continued*)

(b)

FIGURE 17.2 (Continued)   (a–c) A press report on the making of *El mono relojero*.   (*Continued*)

(c)

FIGURE 17.2 (Continued) (a–c) A press report on the making of *El mono relojero.*

technique, animation with cut-out figures, but the public seemed to like only the new style. To work better with cel, he had built animation tables with opaque glass illuminated from underneath, which could rotate on the worktop. This device made the inbetweener's work easier and more comfortable.*

Even though there were no explicit personality conflicts between members of such a numerous crew working on one short film, there were undoubtedly conflicts regarding style. Cristiani wrote:

> I would have liked to adapt the likeable monkey for the screen myself, but Mr. Constancio wanted Ribas to create it. He was a very good artist and very popular in Spain. Mr. Constancio said it would make the film more prestigious. It was the same thing that happened with El Apóstol, however at that time I was able to correct Taborda's drawing to make it more amiable, but in this case, Vigil did not allow me to do so. I had to accept this model, which I liked very much but—just between you and me—it was not the monkey from Vigil's story.

There is no doubt that the most serious contrast was between two forms of inspiration, two creative minds: Cristiani on one side and Vigil on the other. *El mono relojero* kept only the first part of the story's plot. The monkey endures captivity, escapes to the forest, meets animals, and tries in vain to sell them watches. Then he is forced to run away and goes back to his owner. The movie does not have the long chain of errors that lead the literary character to his mortification. The movie character is no more than a disobedient child who runs away and then comes back home again. The funny,

---

* These tables are still used today wherever digital animation has not taken over. They are still the basic work tool for making animated works with animated drawings. Moreover, regarding the *inbetweeners*: at the Cristiani Studio, women were primarily employed in this role. In the USA, however, the position was held exclusively by young men who were practicing their craft to become animators, while women did the cleanup and coloring work.

carefree world of Cristiani was in line with a similar outlook, and there are some successfully comical moments in the film that prove this, but the plot faltered after the main character was modified— because it had been based on the original one (Figure 17.3a–c).

This makes the screenplay seem not very movie-like and rather flat. The movie, as a consequence, lacks suitable development and timing to win the spectators attention. The responsibility for this must be attributed to the adapter, Eleazar P. Maestre, but without exaggerating. This is a personality issue—not a technical issue. Being an uncurable *bohemio*, Cristiani found himself working with

(a)

FIGURE 17.3   (a–c) Advertisement leaflet of the short film *El mono relojero*.
(*Continued*)

(b)

FIGURE 17.3 (Continued)   (a–c) Advertisement leaflet of the short film *El mono relojero*.   (*Continued*)

(c)

FIGURE 17.3 (Continued)   (a–c) Advertisement leaflet of the short film *El mono relojero*.

an austere civil thinker and he did not share or understand the way the man thought about ethics and education. Making fun of the powerful, teasing the politicians, and fresh good-natured irreverence were all characteristics of Cristiani's movies, but they did not fit well in the contest of *Mono relojero*. On one hand, Cristiani was not able to change the story into a *féerie*, but on the other, the producer did not see the subtleties of his work transferred to the screen. The film, in the end, was the result of a compromise.

Even as it is, this film has good qualities. The animation is fluid, the images are detailed, and certain characters were brilliantly imagined (the rhinoceros comes to mind, wearing a surreal metal armor). In several places, the comic author's biting sense of humor comes out. If we want to evaluate it, the film could be considered of average quality, and could stand comparison with any other similar product of its time (Figure 17.4a–f).

(a)

(b)

FIGURE 17.4 (a–f) Some images from *El mono relojero*, which show that the style was influenced by American cartoons and comic strips. This was in contrast with the severe, pedagogic tone that the author, Constancio C. Vigil, had given his story.   (*Continued*)

(c)

(d)

FIGURE 17.4 (Continued) (a–f) Some images from *El mono relojero*, which show that the style was influenced by American cartoons and comic strips. This was in contrast with the severe, pedagogic tone that the author, Constancio C. Vigil, had given his story. (*Continued*)

(e)

(f)

FIGURE 17.4 (Continued) (a–f) Some images from *El mono relojero*, which show that the style was influenced by American cartoons and comic strips. This was in contrast with the severe, pedagogic tone that the author, Constancio C. Vigil, had given his story.

FIGURE 17.5 Quirino Cristiani accepts the first Buenos Aires Municipalidad Film Award from the city's mayor, Carlos A. Pueyrredón.

The Buenos Aires Municipalidad appreciated the film and rewarded it with its first cinema award. Cristiani was always very proud of a photograph that showed him receiving the award from the mayor of Buenos Aires, Carlos A. Pueyrredón. *El mono relojero* was presented to the public on February 10, 1938 at the Cine Monumental, with excellent results (Figure 17.5).

REFERENCES

Cristiani, Q. (1917). *El Apóstol.*
Cristiani, Q. (1931). *Peludópolis.*
Cristiani, Q. (1938). *El mono relojero.*

CHAPTER 18

The Pioneer from Santa Giuletta and the Wizard from Burbank

THE YEAR 1938 PRACTICALLY marked the close of Quirino Cristiani's creative parable. He continued to make amateurishly short films for another four or five years, but he did it in his spare time and worked on subjects that he liked most.

The Argentinean cinema industry had undergone profound changes during the 1930s. More films were being produced, and production companies had merged, growing to industrial sizes with industrial mentalities. Argentina supplied movies for the entire Spanish language market. The allure of the tango; the charisma of actors such as Libertad Lamarque, Luis Sandrini, Floren Delbene, and José Gola; and the prestige of directors such as

Mario Soffici, José A. Ferreyra, and Leopoldo Torres Rios were known beyond their national borders.

In 1931, it had still been possible for Cristiani, a home-based artisan, to present a feature length film conceived only for the people living in the capital, which he had financed and distributed himself; but the situation had changed dramatically in 1938. On the playing field of large investments and international distribution contracts, Cristiani would have been like "a clay jar in the mid of iron vessels" (a vulnerable person who must deal with powerful competitors). The political situation was also not very appealing, for a person who liked to poke fun ("tomar el pelo") at those in power. Since the election of Justo, the situation remained undefined, without impressive personalities. There were alternating situations: compromises, pressure from the armed forces, unnerving maneuvers … until 1945, when Juan Domingo Perón reached the Casa Rosada. And to tell the truth, it was no longer possible to make a vignette-film based on the current events with the equipment available. Animation on cel was far too slow and too costly. With the Lowe brothers competing on the advertising market, it was also very difficult to guarantee the studio's level of earnings. Cristiani decided that it was time for a change, and began to dedicate his talent to a developing, printing, and sound company.

When Dante Quinterno decided to switch from comic strips to cinema and to begin making *Upa en apuros* ("Upa in trouble": Upa is one of the characters in Quinterno's famous comic strip about the native Patoruzú), Cristiani was happy to sell him machinery and equipment. He kept a minimal part of his equipment just not to abandon the sector altogether. In 1941, *Entre pitos y flautas* ("Between whistles and flutes;" but in Spanish there is an allusion to the saying "por pitos o por flautas," which means "for one reason or another") won the Buenos Aires Municipalidad cinema award (Figure 18.1a and b).

(a)

FIGURE 18.1 (a,b) Images from *Entre pitos y flautas*, which won the award from the Buenos Aires Municipalidad in 1941. Cristiani described it as being done with cut-out figures, but these photos show that instead it had been drawn on cel. *(Continued)*

(b)

FIGURE 18.1 (Continued) (a,b) Images from *Entre pitos y flautas*, which won the award from the Buenos Aires Municipalidad in 1941. Cristiani described it as being done with cut-out figures, but these photos show that instead it had been drawn on cel.

In 1943, the same award was given to *Carbonada* ("Mixed dish").

> Cristiani wrote, "Those were two unimportant short films without screenplays. I got the materials from my old productions (cut-out sewn-together figurines), I would choose a few—the funniest ones—and set them one in front of the other as if they were talking together and then I would sit in front of the worktable and film as I "invented" comedy dialogs. They were animated jokes, and one joke had no connection to the next. I did them with different characters. The purpose was to make people laugh. Regarding the title, in Creole a *carbonada* is a mixed salad made with all kinds of ingredients.[*] *Entre pitos y flautas* is about a football match. Here, also, I was making it up on the spot (and without giving it too much

---

[*] More precisely, it is a dish made with different types of cooked vegetables, cooked fruits, rice, corn, potatoes, meat, and other ingredients.

thought). I created playful situations, similar to those that happen in real life during very competitive matches.

The reader should remember that, even though Cristiani clearly stated many times (not just on this occasion) that he had chosen to work with the old cut-out figures for that film, certainly at least *Entre pitos y flautas* was made on cel. We can express an opinion about this film because a few photographs remained.

Two other titles can be mentioned, despite uncertainty and incomplete information. *Buen humor* seems to have also received the award from the city of Buenos Aires, but there are no other details. We can mention *El chiste animado* ("The animated joke"), but it is legitimate to even doubt that it ever existed.

In 1941, Walt Disney visited Argentina. For the United States government, the Hollywood production companies and Mickey Mouse's creator, that was a difficult time indeed. World War II had been raging in Europe for two years already, and it was necessary and urgent to make or recover alliances and look for markets in Latin America. Disney's main problem was private: his animators had started a harsh strike, which he took personally and became exasperated. To find an escape from the situation at home, he had accepted Washington's suggestion to take a goodwill tour of South America as a "flying ambassador." (The strike was resolved while he was away.) Smiling, very friendly, and loved by moviegoers all over the globe, Disney was the right man to help the United States establish the friendly image that it wanted and open business channels. His trip was a personal and political success. Disney used his notes and drawings, made in different places, to make two movies: *Saludos Amigos* and *The Three Caballeros*.

In Buenos Aires, the world's most famous animator met Argentina's most famous animator. Cristiani admired Disney, and he was enthusiastic about meeting him (Figure 18.2).

FIGURE 18.2 Walt Disney in Buenos Aires in 1941, with Quirino Cristiani. In early 1941, before U.S. entry into World War II, the United States Department of State had commissioned a Disney goodwill tour of South America, as part of the Good Neighbour Policy. The tour took ten weeks. Walt Disney, his wife Lilly, and a group of artists and composers from the company visited Brazil, Argentina, Chile, and Peru. Disney was 40 years old, Cristiani was 45 years old.

Cristiani wrote, "Disney's desire was to meet the only artist who did animated drawings in South America. I showed him one of my films at the editing machine (on another occasion, he said that he showed Disney a few parts of *Peludópolis*). He was very impressed and he asked me to come to the United States with him, on his airplane, with a contract as director of animation for some films with a gaucho theme. I thanked him for the honor that he showed me, but I refused. I explained that I love my country very much. In exchange, I introduced him to Molina

Campos, an excellent artist who, though he did not know the technique of animated films, made wonderful caricatures of our *gauchos*. Disney hired him, and with his collaboration made that wonderful film, *Saludos Amigos*, which is based on South American themes and in particular, on the *gauchos* of the Argentinean *Pampas*.

As usual, the director's recollections need to be amended.

Molina Campos˙ was hired by Disney as a consultant in 1942, independently from any Cristiani's intervention.

J. B. Kaufman (2009) adds: "John Rose's daily notes indicate that Cristiani called on Monday, 22 September [1941], and that Jack Cutting went to meet him at his studio." John Rose was the business manager of the touring Disney group. Jack Cutting (1908–1988) joined Disney in 1921 as an animator, and was appointed as the Head of the Foreign Department in 1938.

With this Disney visit, Cristiani basically ended his actual involvement with animated films. But for Argentina—and beyond—his work had been priceless.

REFERENCES

Cristiani, Q. (1931). *Peludópolis*.
Cristiani, Q. (1941). *Entre pitos y flautas*.
Davison, T. (1942). *Upa en apuros*.
Ferguson, N. (1944). *The Three Caballeros*.
Jackson, W., J. Kinney, H. Luske, N. Ferguson, and B. Roberts. (1942). *Saludos Amigos*.
Kaufman, J. B. (2009). *South of the Border with Disney—Walt Disney and the Good Neighbor Program, 1941–1948*, Walt Disney Family Foundation Press, Disney Editions, New York, p. 46n.

˙ Painter and illustrator Florencio Molina Campos (1891–1959) was to the *pampa* and the *gauchos* what Frederic Remington was to the Wild West and the cow boys. He helped shaping the Disney shorts *Goofy Goes Gaucho* and *The Flying Gaucho*, and the feature film *Saludos Amigos*.

CHAPTER 19

Cristiani's Legacy

JUAN OLIVA WAS BORN in Organyá, Catalonia, in 1910, and moved to Argentina as a teenager. When he was about 20, he became a caricature artist for newspapers and magazines, and a comic strip author. In 1932–1933, he joined Cristiani's studio, and while he was working there, he drew and animated about a dozen short film advertisements. In 1938, he was one of the chief animators for the film *El Mono Relojero*. In 1939, Oliva struck out on his own and founded Compañía Argentina de Dibujos Animados. Under this name, he made the short film *La caza al puma* ("Hunting the puma"). The movie was presented to the public in 1940, and was successful. Later, after closing his company, he joined Emelco, the company owned by the Lowe brothers. Here, he started the animated drawings department, and began his teaching career. In 1942, he presented another short film, *Filipito el pistolero,* which he produced himself. He had made it with a small team of collaborators—only four people. From the 1940s until the time of his death in 1975, Oliva split his time between animated cinema, painting (in this field he obtained flattering reviews), and teaching. Students of this student of Cristiani became the cornerstones of Argentinean animation of the 1950s and 1960s.

Dante Quinterno (born: San Vicente, October 26, 1909; died: Buenos Aires, May 14, 2003) worked with Cristiani and then went to the United States to perfect his craft working for the Fleischer brothers. He came back with a project for a color feature film, with two American animators stolen from the Fleischers. That movie was the aforementioned *Upa en apuros*, for which he bought the machinery from his first teacher. The project was carefully prepared and well funded, but specific circumstances prevented him from making it into a feature because the film that he decided to use, Gasparcolor, was produced in Germany and WWII made exports impossible. Quinterno refigured the project, and made the idea into a 16 minute short film in 1942. It was very good, but, strangely, not accepted well by the public.

Another collaborator in advertizing and in the *Mono relojero* was Kayser. He was of German descent (Cristiani believed) and had arrived in South America as an adult. There is no other news about this. Historically speaking, though, Kayser was the pseudonym of Bogoslav Petanjek, a Croat born in Varazdin in 1890 in the Austria–Hungary Empire. He had made his mark as a good caricaturist in Zagreb in the 1920s, and came to Argentina in 1929. Petanjek–Kayser worked with Cristiani for roughly 10 years, and then went to other production companies until he decided to go back to his own country in 1948. He settled in Zagreb, where drawing was a highly respected tradition and there were newly emerging initiatives in the field of animated drawings. He worked on various projects and also finished, in 1949, a 17-minute film called *Misko,* which was never endowed with sound. The interesting thing is that whole sequence of this film was made based on scenes from *Mono relojero,* simply by replacing the monkey with the new main character. Petanjek's technical ability was obviously an example for young animators in his area. Less than 10 years later, they opened the internationally acclaimed Zagreb School of Animated Films. Petanjek retired in 1957 and died in 1978.

Artistically speaking, these were the direct heirs of Quirino Cristiani. His spiritual heirs were those who made animated films in Argentina from the 1940s onward.

José M. Burone Bruché, Oliva's successor at Emelco in 1942, made *Consejos del viejo Vizcacha* (in 1945, in color, with Alexcolor's signature procedure).

Jorge Caro became known for *Puños de campeón* in the 1950s.

Leonardo Goilemberg and Carlos Gonzáles Groppa did puppet animation in the 1950s.

Victor A. Iturralde Rúa, a man with many interests, made movies painted on film in the 1950s together with Leon Herman.

Manuel Garcia Ferré was the author of various feature films during the 1960s and 1970s.

Gil & Bertolini and many others followed in Cristiani's footsteps in the field of animated advertisements.

Jorge Martin (*alias* Catú) directed 260 short films starring Mafalda, the little girl invented by Quino (Joaquín Lavado) for a comic strip.

Simón Feldman, a painter, debuted in 1959 as a film director with a "live-action" political satire movie *El negoción* ("The deal"), and in 1976 presented a feature film with animated drawings called *Los cuatro secretos* ("The four secrets").

Finally, Oscar Grillo, who is probably the best living animator with an Argentinean passport, works in Great Britain and won the Golden Palm at the Cannes Film Festival in 1980 for his short film, *Seaside Woman*.

Quirino Cristiani retired in 1961. In 1977, the Buenos Aires Municipalidad honored him during the celebration to mark the eightieth anniversary of Argentinean cinema. In 1981, General Jorge Videla, the *de facto* president at that time, gave him a lifetime pension as recognition for his work as a pioneer in the field of animation, and the postal service printed a stamp in his honor (Figure 19.1a–d).

On November 29, 1981, accompanied by his son, Atilio, he went back to visit Santa Giuletta after an official invitation from the

(a)

(b)

FIGURE 19.1 (a–d) Headshots of Quirino Cristiani on his return to Santa Giuletta (Italy), his home town. On November 29, 1981, the Municipality of Santa Giuletta and the Administration of the Province of Pavia gave a reception to welcome Cristiani back. He was returning to Italy 80 years after his emigration. (*Continued*)

(c)

(d)

FIGURE 19.1 (Continued) (a–d) Headshots of Quirino Cristiani on his return to Santa Giuletta (Italy), his home town. On November 29, 1981, the Municipality of Santa Giuletta and the Administration of the Province of Pavia gave a reception to welcome Cristiani back. He was returning to Italy 80 years after his emigration.

local municipality and the Province of Pavia. He was honored with celebrations and acknowledgments. It was the first time he had been back to Italy, and his first time on an airplane. On that occasion, he collected a bit of soil to take back to Argentina, saying "Para mí esto es sagrado" ("this is a holy thing to me") to justify the old-fashioned gesture.

Quirino Cristiani died serenely in his sleep in Bernal on August 2, 1984, aged 88 (Figure 19.2).

FIGURE 19.2 Quirino Cristiani in a caricature drawn by Gabriele Zucchelli, the animator who directed and produced the first documentary on him.

REFERENCES

Cristiani, Q. (1938). *El mono relojero.*

Davison, T. (1942). *Upa en apuros.*

Feldman, S. (1959). *El negoción.*

Feldman, S. (1976). *Los cuatro secretos.*

Appendix 1: Historical Notes

F ROM AN INSTITUTIONAL STANDPOINT, during the time period spanning the turn of the twentieth century, Argentina was a liberal democracy based on a federal constitution, similar to that of the United States. The president was the head of the government: he served a six-year term and could be reelected, but not for a consecutive term.

But the style of government was more "liberist" than "liberalist," and there were few traces of true democracy. A rich Criollo oligarchy held power and was able to use falsifications and intimidation to influence the outcome of elections. As the massive flow of immigrants into Argentina changed its social, racial, and anthropological make up, this elite circle tightened on itself. The governing class saw themselves as aristocrats in relation to the heterogeneous masses that formed different classes and ethnic groups, each of which trying to maintain its own culture of origin and turning a deaf ear to the nation's old and new problems unless they were directly involved. The Criollo oligarchy worried about themselves, and their representatives devoted their time to two typically aristocratic pleasures: politics and enjoying life.

The Partido Autonomista Nacional supported these conservatives, and chose the presidents elected from 1880 to 1916.

The policy of this era was to open up to foreign investments, especially British, to aid exports of grain and frozen meat (the first refrigerators were installed in 1883) as well as to build infrastructures such as harbors and railroads. Social conflict was repressed. Access to power for the petty and middle bourgeoisie (not to mention the lower working class) was impossible. The conservatives' biggest error was probably that they did not understand what kind of country was forming with the transformations that they had sponsored. The newly created social groups defined themselves in nontraditional ways. At the beginning of the twentieth century, the middle class and the working class were so numerous that only the blindness of those who were determined to self-destruct could prevent them from being seen.

In 1890, a socialist association of German workers proposed an international committee to organize a May 1 Labor Day celebration in Buenos Aires. More or less during the same time period, the opposition of the Partido Autonomista Nacional gathered to find another group, the Unión Cívica party. Leandro N. Alem was its president. Unión Cívica could count on support from certain groups: young citizens, those who had lost faith in the oligarchy and certain Catholic factions. On July 26, 1890, they started a revolt with the support of a few military groups, but it was suffocated after an initial success. The party split two years later during the election: the Unión Cívica Nacional on one side, and the Unión Cívica Radical on the other, led by Alem. The first party fit the description of the traditional oligarchic politics (its leader, Bartolomé Mitre, quickly made a deal with the leader of the conservatives, Julio A. Roca), and the second party proved to be a truly new party: the people's party, which represented the emerging middle classes.

In 1893, the radicals sponsored another insurrection, and they failed this time also. This was when Hipólito Yrigoyen, nephew of Leandro N. Alem, first emerged. When Alem committed suicide in 1895, Yrigoyen became the charismatic leader of the party and of all Argentineans who wanted a different model of society.

In the meantime, Argentina was facing the serious issue of defining its borders with Chile. The risk of war could be felt, and the emergency situation brought Julio A. Roca back to the presidency. He was the party leader, and had been president from 1880 to 1886. The Argentine–Chilean crisis was resolved in 1902, thanks to an arbitration of King Edward VII of England, but nevertheless, left its mark on the country's internal politics. The minister of war, Colonel Pablo Riccheri, took advantage of the occasion to finalize reforms modernizing the armed forces. He submitted a plan to the Congress, which included a mandatory draft, and focused his strength on achieving a politically neutral army of professional soldiers. The plan became a law in 1901.

Economic development continued, and so did the hostility between the political currents in power. In 1905, Argentineans found themselves in another crisis. Hipólito Yrigoyen's radicals started another revolt in the capital and the provinces. Radicalism had enlarged its base: rural areas, which no longer tolerated the omnipotence of rich landowners, old enemies of Roca who had been fooled by the liberal Bartolomé Mitre, and vast numbers of former immigrants who were now part of the Argentinean population. However, radicalism had not been able to influence the smaller working class that ascribed to the socialist and anarchic ideas. The revolt of 1905 was repressed. Many were jailed and deported, and the government did not waste the chance to persecute the radicals and the representatives of the labor movement. Yrigoyen was able to escape his adversaries for months, and this allowed him to live with the people and discover first hand just how strongly they supported his plan for change and him as a person. On the other side, the conservatives were exhausted. The governor of Buenos Aires, Marcelino Ugarte, was intransigent in supporting Roca and used all his power to support hard, reactionary governments and candidates, but other conservatives, such as

Carlos Pellegrini and Roque Sáenz-Peña, looked ahead and tried to talk to the progressives.

Roque Sáenz-Peña became president in October of 1910. In January 1911 he sent his plan for a new electoral law to Congress, which met for a special session. In February 1912, the law was promulgated: it involved a universal free secret vote, minority representation, and rigorous controls to assure correct practice in operations by the judicial authorities. From then on, the law was simply referred to as "la Sáenz-Peña." It was tried out right away at the elections of March 1912, when Argentineans in the Santa Fé province went to the polls to elect their governor. The radicals won by a landslide. It was clear that when Sáenz-Peña finished his term, the winning candidate would be the one chosen by the only party truly supported by the majority of the population. Sáenz-Peña died on August 9, 1914, and his term was concluded by his vice president, Victorino de la Plaza, an honest man who was not above aspiring for nationalistic patriotism (because of the need for new foreign markets to compete with the British market). Victorino de la Plaza was anyway a rather quiet leader, whose most important act as president was to declare his country's neutrality when the World War I broke out.

On April 2, 1916 Hipólito Yrigoyen was elected president with more than 350,000 votes against the 250,000 votes of the other parties, which included the conservatives, progressive democrats, and socialists. On October 12, the day he was to take office, the people of Buenos Aires gathered in the streets to cheer the first radical president. On the road between the Congress building and the Casa de Gobierno, the multitude unhitched the horses from the presidential coach and pulled it to its destination. Leading this show of support were the sons of middle class businessmen who had been shunned by wealthy bankers and landowners, and representatives of the immigrants that had come over during the past 30 years.

The country's hopes were high, and Yrigoyen had done nothing to diminish them before he took office. Moreover, he had launched strong accusations of corruption and blind greed against conservative politicians. He and his supporters had come to build a new type of Argentina, but with the possibilities of many *intervenciones* (the best translation would be "compulsory administration," at least in a juridical sense) of provinces with conservative governments, which many people said would happen; the new president became very cautious.

"The Unión Cívica Radical party did not come to the government to *punish*, but to *repair*," said the president in a speech. This was the goal of a simple but calculated political move: To do his best to avoid any friction during the change of power, knowing full well that the adversary continued to control the economical and financial monopoly, command the majority in Parliament, and enjoy wide approval among the armed forces and connections with large economic interests abroad. When the air cleared, of course, Yrigoyen did not hold back from using the *intervención* as a tool: at the end of his terms in office, he had enacted 20.

At least one happened immediately: It happened in the province of Buenos Aires itself, which ended the black heart of conservatism and ousted Marcelino Ugarte (1885–1929) during his second term. He had been governor from 1902 to 1904, and was reelected in 1914.

"He was a great conservative," recalled Quirino Cristiani, "and he did not agree with Yrigoyen, who was exactly the opposite. The *intervención* was carried out by José Luis Cantilo, then the mayor (intendente) of the city of Buenos Aires."*

Hipólito Yrigoyen (the Creole pronunciation is *irigòzhen*) was born on July 12, 1852 in Buenos Aires, to a family of landowners of Basque descent. He had always been attracted to politics—at the age of 26 he was elected deputy of the province of Buenos Aires—and the example set by his uncle Leandro N. Alem had motivated him to join the Unión Cívica party.

---

* Readers should know that the city of Buenos Aires is not part of the province of the same name. The national capital is juridically autonomous. The capital of the province of Buenos Aires is the small city of La Plata.

Though he was rich (it is said that he sold more than two million pesos worth of property to support the party), he was not arrogant or despotic, and he was a mediator instead of a despotic leader. He was Argentina's first example of the European-style politician, which was defined in the 1900s as "a man responsible to a party organization, responsible before the changing demands of the electorate, conditioned by the former and the latter but also able to condition them, capable of maneuvering and a pragmatic decision-maker." Yrigoyen was probably better as a party leader than as head of state. His ability to listen to the requests of various groups and the *caciques*, the local territorial or family-based clan leaders, allowed him to fortify the Unión Cívica Radical anywhere in the country, transforming it into a group of illuminated liberals in a popular, modern party with a populist ideology.

Yrigoyen's real personality was always difficult to understand. He was an austere man, but did not oppose the corruption that soon developed within his party and his administration. His moral rigor (for decades he refused the proposals from the oligarchic club for honors and ministers, and kept his party in a position of electoral abstention until he obtained a universal voting law) earned him unconditioned respect for the petty bourgeoisie. However, he also astutely used his influence and conspiracy tactics to win. To show his detachment from his original social class, he did not hesitate to change his last name. His original surname started with an I. He chose to spell it with a Y, and this difference became almost a sign of a choice: to the point that his conservative adversaries used his original surname in their attacks against him.

However, it is impossible to construct a credible profile of Yrigoyen. His biographers have interpreted his political actions in different (sometimes totally contrasting) ways, but his words remain indecipherable. A charismatic man, he enjoyed the gift of incommunicability. He did not love crowds, nor did he encourage them as other leaders did (such as Juan Domingo Perón, to cite another Argentinean). His speeches were hermetic and gave him the feel of a "Doctor," a man who understood what others could not grasp.

This widespread hermeticism was perhaps the basis of the curious nickname that he was known by for his entire public life, "El Peludo." The Creole language word *peludo* means armadillo, an animal with a bony armor that can make it invulnerable when it rolls up in a ball.

The sense of being closed, physically or psychologically, is the basis for the nickname. According to others, more realistically, the term was derogatory—coined by aristocrats to denote vulgarity or unpleasantness, or a lower social class (the first meaning of *peludo* was "hairy" in Spanish). Quirino Cristiani reasoned candidly that the name came from the fact that Yrigoyen had a lot of hair: "tenía mucho pelo, molti capelli."

The new president was showered with caricatures. He did not have a haughty disposition and the Argentinean tradition, unlike that of other Latin American countries, was such that a tetchy leader would have difficulty finding enough material and moral resources to shut his opposers up. In particular, Yrigoyen showed no reaction to *El Apóstol* or its director, even though Cristiani liked to tell people (and himself) that the president had also laughed at the film, and talked with his friends about "that crazy artist."

Cristiani remembered Yrigoyen as follows:

> He was a good president, a great man, and a man of great sentiment. A democratic man. The Argentinean people are indebted to him for not entering the First World War, even though the military pressured him to do so.

When he rose to power in 1916, Hipólito Yrigoyen finished his first term in 1922 at the age of 70. An elated public had initially elected him, and he left the Casa Rosada with still greater prestige, though his government had been contradictory and not impeccable. In the economical sector, he promoted cautious government intervention, which contradicted the pure liberist doctrine of the conservatives. Socially, he introduced the eight-hour workday and made Sunday a mandatory day of rest. He promoted popular housing, and established mandatory insurance for workers. Yrigoyen developed a more nationalistic attitude than his predecessors and opposers, and opposed the omnipotence of foreign money in Argentina. He also supported reforms in schools and universities: the latter happened after student demonstrations in May 1918 at the University of Córdoba. However, the structure and ideology of the liberal state were not touched: they were only adapted and smoothed over.

"Yrigoyen's great error was putting aside the political platform that the people had voted for, which included using federal intervention procedures in all provinces and a call to general elections in which the people's decision clearly emerged," wrote Fermín Chavez, a historian with a radical perspective. "Forgiving the past ended up being nothing more than forgiving the old regime."

According to purists of the radical movement, Yrigoyen was supposed to embody the spirit of the Argentinean masses, which would always have been hostile to the constitution (and therefore to liberalism) each time that they were allowed to participate in public life. He would have had to "purify" the State (we should remember that this was the very reason he was ridiculed in *El Apóstol*) to change the government all the way through. The idea was to start the revolution at the top instead of from the grass root level.

Instead, he accepted the institutions setup by the conservative regime: the provincial governments, parliament, and— especially—the economic structures that the old oligarchy was based on. Perhaps he was not bold enough, but he was certainly not the head of a party that could sustain him properly. The intellectuals of radicalism were almost all liberals, who did not feel comfortable countering the form and spirit of the constitution. The party was deeply divided into factions, and was made up of formerly marginal groups that aspired to fit into the establishment instead of changing it. Finally, and maybe most importantly, radicalism did not have an ideological vision. Normally, when groups without a definite ideology come to power, the newly elected opposition leaders act just like the old regime when it comes to decision-making, and this is exactly what happened to the radicalists. In fact, most of the time, they were even worse than the conservatives. For many, being elected to the government meant a social promotion and the acquisition of money and power.

In 1917, the Russian revolution broke out and its effects were also felt in the southern hemisphere. Strikes started to become more frequent and more harsh, and the economic situation favored the tension because the emergency industries that opened during the war (which had blocked imports) were being squelched. Labor was also in difficulty, but prices were climbing and actual salaries were dwindling. In January 1919, Buenos Aires was hit by a strike that soon turned into an authentic insurrection, instigated by the anarchics. Yrigoyen appointed General Luís Dellepiane as the city's military governor, and the week that is defined "the tragic week" in the history books ended with hundreds of victims. The president appeared indecisive and faltering, and neither the reactionaries nor the progressives forgave him.

But Yrigoyen's worst error, from a long-term perspective, was his interaction with the military. Based on reforms backed by General Riccheri, the Argentinean armed forces were supposed to have a rigorously professional structure, detached from political parties and election-related problems. But Yrigoyen could not conceive of armed forces which were not a supporting factor for his cause and his republic. After decades of plotting uprisings and involving as many officers as possible, he did not realize that uniformed soldiers were supposed to be a power separate from the executive branch. For a long time, he courted them to get them to join the radicalist movement. In addition, his nonmilitarist attitude (not really antimilitarist), which actually means a complete lack of comprehension of the military mentality, brought him to a more pronounced detachment, which resulted in surprising instances of tactlessness.

During his first presidency, he committed a number of gaffes without even realizing it.

First of all, the military did not approve of his appointment of Elpidio González, a civilian, as the Minister of War. That position was traditionally held by a general. The minister (one of the president's faithful men) managed promotions and movements of officers arbitrarily, on the basis of a patronage system. In addition, the armed forces did not get adequate financing to update their equipment, and during Peludo's entire presidency, they never had to perform large-scale operations. In 1922, officials who had been expelled from the army for taking part in radical uprisings in 1890, 1893, and 1905 were reinstated. The reinstatement did not have practical effects, but it had upset the people.

The straw that broke the camel's back was the president's decision to use the navy or the army to quell the worker's revolts that broke out in different places in the country during the latter years of his term. Up to then, the police had been employed to repress public demonstrations. Soldiers were repulsed by the idea of being deployed in a civil war, and they were even more sickened when they found themselves fighting side by side with private militia hired by the company owners to fight the demonstrators.

The Unión Cívica Radical arrived at the 1922 elections with a very fragile internal structure. Their designated candidate was Marcelo Torcuato de Alvear (1868–1942), one of the radical party's earliest members, who belonged to the moderate–liberal branch of the party (the "top-hats" known as *galeritas*). The vice-presidential candidate Elpidio González balanced the formula and satisfied strict Yrigoyen supporters. Disagreements did not prevent success at the urns. The radical candidates won with more than 450,000 votes, against the 200,000 votes cast for conservatives and a marginal number of votes that went to the Partido Democrata Progresista, the Partido Socialista, and the Unión Cívica Radical Principista.

Alvear, a good politician who learned much in Europe (he was Yrigoyen's ambassador to Paris), led the country with moderation and sobriety, both in internal and foreign policy. The country prospered during his term. There were no social or institutional changes under his leadership either. The radical president governed the nation similar to a prudent conservative. Elpidio González never had the chance to do anything: Alvear never decided to use his constitutional right to delegate power, for a limited time, to his second-in-command. Instead, the man who had power during his presidency was Agustín P. Justo, a clever liberal with a military career who had a lot of followers in the armed forces. He was appointed Minister of War, and during the six years that he led the ministry, he prepared for his own future presidency along with the military overthrow of 1930. First of all, he cultivated his relationship with radical *antipersonalistas*, in the name of a large percentage of the armed forces. Actually, most of the servicemen were not in favor of radical fractionists as much as they were against Yrigoyen running for president again and the power that men in his government would have. They did not want people such as Elpidio González or General Luís Dellepiane, the ex-military governor of Buenos Aires during the "tragic week" and loyal defender of the radical republic, to have such power. Alvear, on the other hand, had strong ties to the *antipersonalistas,* but he was careful to remain above the political skirmishes and prepared himself to return to Paris as soon as his six-year term expired.

In 1928, the *antipersonalistas* nominated Leopoldo Melo and Vicente Gallo as president and vice president, respectively. The *personalistas* did not let Yrigoyen's age bother them, and they nominated him (he was 76, but seemed much older).

The elections were held on April 1, 1928. The older candidate won hands down, winning twice the number of votes as the *antipersonalista* pair: 839,140 against 439,178. For the people, nothing had changed: "Peludo" was still their apostle. He was no longer a mere politician—he was a living legend. On October 12, 1928, his glory reached its zenith: his second term inauguration took place in the mid of a vast crowd. But the situation soon revealed itself to be very different from what voters had imagined. Yrigoyen was no longer able to tell a small problem from a large issue, and his faith in his collaborators had turned into the naivety of old age. The 1929 stock market crash sent shock waves through the economy of the entire industrialized world, and the Argentinean economy suffered especially due to the country's raw materials exports. Certain political assassinations brought the internal situation to a white hot level of tension. The government proved incapable of managing these emergencies, and also failed to ensure ordinary administration. The country found itself with no one at the helm. The president's opponents, from the *antipersonalistas* to the conservatives, attacked him from every side and with everything they could think of—from conspiracy theories to accusations in the media. *Crítica*, a very aggressive morning newspaper with a vast circulation, was the *antipersonalistas'* most authoritative and effective arena.

Jokes and gossip abounded, and the government's credibility crumbled with each passing day. Corruption and favoritism had increased over 30 years of radical leadership, and the average citizen was thoroughly exasperated.

The nicest thing that was said about the man living in the Casa Rosada was that he was not so much guilty as he was a victim of collaborators and ministers who lied to him to achieve their own ends. Sustainers of this idea believed that the liars even went so far as to provide falsified copies of the newspapers to make him believe that the people were happy and that everything was fine. Oddly enough, similar stories of "the great leader misguided by his inner circle" also emerged later with other leaders, including Mussolini and Perón.

The government was not governing, but it did devote a lot of energy to internal conflict. As time went by, it became more and more probable that President Yrigoyen would die in office, and therefore the race was on for his successor. Vice president Enrique Martínez, supported by the current Minister of the Interior,

Elpidio González, was on one side. Their intention was to ask Yrigoyen to resign, and one of them would become president, whereas the other would be the old leader's spiritual heir. Their aim was bent on their egotistic desires to continue their political careers, but this was nonetheless the most forward-looking option: Their election would have allowed them to salvage what was left of the administration's original prestige and setup a reasonably operative government. The other option, formed by the die-hard Yrigoyen supporters, was led by Horacio B. Oyhanarte (ideologist, lawyer, and writer), who managed Argentina's foreign politics.

Two different trains of thought conspired against these two options. One of these pooled the *antipersonalistas*, the conservatives, and the independent socialists (which, despite their name, were also conservative in nature). This group simply wanted to remove the president from office. After a brief military government that would "fix things," they thought that Yrigoyenism would just disappear by itself and Argentina would be like it was before his presidencies. The other conspiracy group was the nationalists. Based on the experience of Italian fascism, the Spanish *paternalista* dictatorship of Miguel Primo de Rivera, and theories of the founder of Action Française, Charles Maurras, certain groups had started to envision a society with an organized hierarchy in which corporatism could replace parliamentary democracy. This vision of totalitarian right-wing government included great ideas of ethical rigor, which preached a sort of asceticism with regard to duty, but serious issues of brutality and militarism. The poet Leopoldo Lugones was one of the movement's theorists. The nationalists also wanted to remove Yrigoyen from office, but for the purpose of doing away with radicalism, liberalism, socialism, and so on.

These were the trends, but the actual facts dictated that only one institution could upend the government: The army.

As his Minister of War, Yrigoyen had appointed General Luís Dellepiane, the sworn enemy of his predecessor Agustín P. Justo.

General Justo had promoted and stationed officers unscrupulously and had dedicated a great deal of attention to consolidating his own power. This had created a great deal of resentment. When the new Minister's personnel took possession of the offices, they threw out everything, even the office supplies—pens, absorbent paper, typing paper, and new envelopes—as if they were contaminated. The resentment was so strong that the minister turned it into an anti-Justo offensive movement, and in a short time the political organization set up by General Justo was attacked and disassembled: More than 60% of the officers were restationed immediately and their orders were changed.

Dellepiane knew how to keep his eyes open. He noticed the preparations (which were not really hidden at all) for the *coup d'etat* that Justo and his men had been planning in collaboration with the nationalists, who were led by General José Félix Uriburu. He requested an audience with Yrigoyen and explained the situation, and urged the president to authorize him to take action. He was surprised to hear the president tell him to be calm and not worry about it. Yrigoyen was a former leader of uprisings, and could not imagine that someone would rise up against him. He had been elected with such a large margin that he did not believe that a few men with weapons could overturn his government against the nation's will. Finally, he disdained soldiers so much that he did not believe they were able to carry out such a mission. He believed that his minister had an overactive imagination, and sent him away.

Elpidio González and Enrique Martínez, convinced that Yrigoyen was the conspiracy's only target, saw Dellepiane's work as an obstacle to their plans, and they started several slanderous rumors against him. Generale Uriburu sent one of his own spokesmen to assure the president that he was not involved in any conspiracy, and to request that the surveillance measures that Dellepiane had ordered against him be removed. Yrigoyen honored the word of a "soldier and man of honor" and ordered to stop the surveillance.

Dellepiane resigned on September 3, 1930. In his place Yrigoyen, who was obviously no longer able to control his own actions, appointed the worst man possible for the job, Elpidio González. On September 5, the president became ill and delegated his presidency to his vice president, Martínez, who acted like he thought he really was the president and tried to remove people who were not his friends from the government. He only managed to provoke a head-to-head collision with the Minster of Foreign Affairs, Oyhanarte. On September 6, the final act took place: Generale Uriburu marched on the Casa Rosada, leading a small but determined group of soldiers.

Justo, who was also in favor of a military takeover, had let the impulsive Uriburu steal the show.

Forces loyal to the government were ready to intervene against Uriburu and they would have been able to defeat the over throwers, but Martínez let the insurrectionists get to the Casa Rosada as his faithful soldiers watched. Martínez was disheartened to hear Uriburu say that the *revolución* was not done to keep him in office—they wanted him out just like all the others. However, until the evening, the situation fluctuated. Elpidio González, with the heads of most of the armed forces, was at the *Arsenale* and always able to react. Justo intervened by delivering Martínez's resignation to the *Arsenale*. A loyalist general, Enrique Mosconi, went to see the resigning vice president to make sure that the document was authentic and to inform him that he could still depend on strong support from the troops. Martínez said to send everyone home. Even Elpidio González raised the white flag, and Yrigoyenism ceased.

The Argentinean people were not enthusiastic about their president being overturned, but they were relieved that the inactive government was out of power. Born as a dream, *El Peludo's* second presidency had turned into a nightmare, and the temporary president Uriburu was better than nothing. Uriburu (in whose lines had marched a young captain from Justo's party named Juan Domingo Perón) formed a government of civilians only, made up of members of the old oligarchy. His plans for a corporate state remained on the drawing board, and he proved to be even less capable of governing than the patriarch that he had defeated. Even though the elections of March 1930 ended in a resounding defeat for the radicals, and students had gathered in Plaza de Mayo to demand Yrigoyen's resignation, eight months after the military coup, voters of the Province of Buenos Aires voted for the radicals again.

The radical vote was so compact and the margin was so wide that it frightened the coup leaders and put an end to the idea of investing in Uriburu and his fascist dreams. At the end of 1931, the temporary president knew he had to leave the Casa Rosada. Elections were held on November 8, and intimidations and quibbling prevented Unión Cívica Radical from participating. The new leader of Argentina became General Agustín P. Justo, candidate of the Concordancia party, the alliance of the conservative wing.

Appendix 2: Cinema, Theater, Radio, and Comics

ARGENTINEAN CINEMA TOOK ON its own shape during the time period encompassing World War I and the years immediately following. The circumstances of war forced internal production to increase, to the point that in 1917 Argentinean companies presented an incredible total of 30 films. New production companies opened, including the Cinematografía in Rio de la Plata, Porteña Film, Ortiz Film, Argentina Film, and Ariel Film. Actors such as Pablo Podestà, Nelo Cosimi, Camila Quiroga, and Silvia Parodi won the hearts of viewers from the big screen after having triumphed on the theater stages. In addition, Antonio Cunill Cabanillas filled the vacuum left by Charlie Chaplin when his new movies could not be imported, with a stunningly accurate imitation of the legendary comedian in *Carlitos en Buenos Aires*.

In 1917, *El tango de la muerte* (Deadly Tango) came out. It was the first effort of José Agustín Ferreyra, a biracial man (nicknamed "Negro" for his skin color) who would go on to establish himself as the best silent filmmaker of his time in Rio de la Plata, using sentimental, popular, and "neorealist" subjects before they became known as actual categories. Ferreyra is indicated by scholars studying Argentinean cinema as the first film director who really understood the typical, autonomous national mindset and successfully communicated it to the viewers. Roberto Guidi (1890–1958) was different. He was a scholar who wrote a movie language manual (one of the world's first) and who sought an intellectual style and refined technique in his five-year long career as a director. His films were *El mentir de los demás* (1919, Other People's Lies), *Mala yerba* (1920, Bad Grass), *Aves de rapiña* (1921, Birds of Prey) and finally, *Escándalo a medianoche* (1923, Scandal at Midnight, from *The Three-cornered Hat* by Pedro Antonio Alarcón). Leopoldo Torres Rios also debuted at that time, but he was destined to become famous in the 1930s. Directors such as the aforementioned Nelo Cosimi, Edmo Cominetti, and Julio Irigoyen (no relation to the president) also emerged. Without belonging to the club of world movie superpowers, Argentina was a power in its own right in the Spanish language market. Based on a strong internal market (theaters in Buenos Aires were among the most beautiful and well-equipped in the entire world; one of the best was Buckingham Palace, which could seat more than 3000 patrons), the industry could concentrate on exporting to other Latin American countries. This laid the foundation for the future economic development of this film industry, which in the 1930s and 1940s would expand and greatly increase production to rival Mexico for first place in the Hispanic American area.

Argentinean entertainment, despite the introduction of cinema productions, continued to claim the theater as its strong point. Actors and stages were traditionally loved by the *porteños,* and playwrights were some of the most visible people in the capital city. During the 1910s, light popular theater developed quickly: comedy made room for the *sainete,* the farce. Often the caricature focused on political life, as was natural for a nation that recognized its own sense of humor. Political life had provided themes for plays and farces as far back as 1879, when Rafael Barrera wrote *La conciliación,* and in 1885 Eduardo Sojo had presented

Don Quijote en Buenos Aires—and the city government closed his theater as a result. Exequiel Soria had used character of the founder of radicalism, Leandro N. Alem, in his work *El año noventa y dos*, and in 1900 he offered the public *Politica casera*. In 1913, Vicente Martinez Cuitiño presented *El Caudillo*; the following year Alberto Vaccarezza repeated his message with *El comité*. The characters of Yrigoyen and Alvear were put on stage or on screen in every imaginable way. In particular, Carlos Ossorio and Carlos Alberto Silva stage play *Don Agenor Saladillo* (1918) made fun of the Yrigoyenist Minister of Justice and Public Education, José Santos Salina; and the atmosphere of Alvear's time was reflected in the *sainete* (one-act comedy) *Conventillo nacional* (1925) by Alberto Vaccarezza. The work of caricaturist and film director Quirino Cristiani fits into this entertainment tradition, as well as the field of drawn political caricatures.

The theater resisted competition from films up until the 1930s. In 1927, it was still thriving: in the capital there were 137 theater performance rooms, 25 in the center alone. In addition, there were also opera theaters. The Colón was one of the world's main opera houses, along with the Scala Theater in Milan and the New York Metropolitan. The Victoria, the Politeama, and the Variedades featured mainly French opera, and the Teatro de la Opera had featured the famous tenor Enrico Caruso since 1899.

Considering radio, a doctor and three very young medical students all fell in love with the new technology and decided to start broadcasting. Their names were Enrique T. Susini, Miguel Mújica, César J. Guerrico, and Luis Romero Carranza. They installed heavy, complicated equipment on the roof of the Coliseo Argentino theater, and on the evening of August 27, 1920 they broadcasted *Parsifal* directed by Weingartner to a small group of listeners in their homes. Yrigoyen, when he learned of the initiative, commented paternalistically, "When young people play at being scientists, it is because there is genius inside them." For two years, the young students that "played scientist" had a monopoly on radio, broadcasting performances from the Coliseo, the

Colón, and the Odeon, as well as news and sports reports of soccer games and performances of popular orchestras and singers. In 1923, a second station opened, Radio Sud America, followed a few months later by a third, Radio Cultura. Then came Lov, Radio Brusa, Radio Libertad, Radio Casa America, Radio Grand Splendid, and Radio Nacional. In 1924, a radio station opened in Rosario and another opened shortly thereafter in Santa Fé. In 1926, a station opened in La Plata, others opened in Mar del Plata and Córdoba in 1927 and in 1928 a second began broadcasting in Rosario. Programs started during early morning hours and went on until after midnight. Men and women radio stars made their fortunes (and lost them) on the air, and advertizing through the "wireless telegraph" became necessary for sales in Argentina.

These few notes would be incomplete without the mention of a branch that cannot be classified as live entertainment, but that is closely related.

The comic strip was introduced in Argentina in 1912, in the magazine *Caras y caretas*. Previously, countless satirical and political vignettes were published by *Rioplatense* publications, dating back to the time of the war for independence.

During the 1870s, the satirical comedy publication *El Mosquito*, founded by Frenchman Henri Meyer, had published politically inspired drawings in a series that told stories. In the 1880s, another publication, *Don Quijote*, had published strips on satirical–political subjects. As it turned out, the artistic path that led to *El Apóstol* and the work of other Argentinean animators in the first decades of the century was similar to a royal road. Artists such as Henri Stein, Manuel Mayol, and José Maria Cao had prepared the way. As regards actual comic strips, in 1912, *Caras y caretas* published the first strips by Manuel Redondo, and the first characters were Viruta and Chicharrón. Their creators are still unknown. In 1913, Redondo was working on Sarrasqueta (drawn at first by Juan Carlos Alonso), a snobbish, prudish Spanish immigrant who observed and commented on customs of the time. In 1916, "Negro Raúl" by Arturo Lanteri was created, a middle class character with frustrated ambitions. In 1923, Lanteri also created a series called the *Aventuras de don Pancho Talero*, a family saga similar to *Bringing up Father* by George McManus. Viruta and Chicharrón were brought to the big screen in a film (not animated) produced before 1920 by Max Glucksmann: *Aventuras de Viruta y Chicharrón*. Pancho Talero was also made into a movie, *Pancho Talero en Hollywood*, which was written, produced, and directed by Arturo Lanteri. It was a silent film with unnamed actors, and was later redone with a sound track and distributed in 1931. Although the spaces reserved for comic strips multiplied in nonspecialized publications, and specialized magazines emerged, Dante Quinterno and his Native American character Patoruzú appeared. Quinterno, soon rich and famous, became a publisher and built a small Disney-style empire.

The final success of comics in Argentina—known as *historietas*—came at the end of the 1920s. Almost all of the big daily newspapers "opened up" to *comics* and published both translated American and national strips. This was the springboard for the race that took Argentinean comics skyrocketing in the 1950s and 1960s, when they were established as being one of the most original and lively comic strip industries in the world.

REFERENCES

Cristiani, Q. (1917). *El Apóstol*.
Guidi, R. (1919). *El mentir de los demás*.
Guidi, R. (1920). *Mala yerba*.
Guidi, R. (1921). *Aves de rapiña*.
Guidi, R. (1923). *Escándalo a medianoche*.
Lanteri, A. (1931). *Pancho Talero en Hollywood*.
Ossorio, C. and C. A. Silva. (1918). *Don Agenor Saladillo*.
Vaccarezza, A. (1925). *Conventillo nacional*.

Appendix 3:
Spurlos Versenkt

IT IS WORTH RECOUNTING the complete story of the sinking of the Argentinean merchant ship in 1917 and the curious reconstruction of events that Quirino Cristiani made of it, at least for the purpose of demonstrating how imprecise the memories of creative people often are, generally speaking, and of filmmakers in particular. Those who have tried to assemble the memoirs of (say) Frank Capra or Charlie Chaplin or Federico Fellini can confirm this.

After having called the sunken ship the "cannoniera Toro" (and in one letter "cannoniera Chaco"), he observed that the origin of the incident was probably to be found in the battle of Rio de la Plata, during which the German ship *Graf Spee*, defeated by the British, sought refuge in an Argentinean harbor and was expelled. On account of that expulsion, the ship was then sunk. According to this line of reasoning, the Germans had sunk the Argentinean ship "without leaving a trace" out of revenge. He added that the sailors on the *Graf Spee* mutinied and then moved into Argentina and were found many years later—married and with children—as the founders of a real city, Colonia Belgrano.

The historical reality is that during World War I, the only naval battle in waters close to Argentina was the Battle of the Falkland Islands on December 8, 1914. On that occasion, German admiral Count Maximilian von Spee (1861–1914) was defeated by the larger British squadron led by Admiral Doveton Sturdee.

Instead, the Battle of Rio de la Plata took place 25 years later, during World War II. The German heavy cruiser (or "pocket battleship") *Admiral Graf Spee*, was fighting short battles in the South Atlantic and was intercepted on December 13, 1939 by the British war ships *Exeter*, *Ajax*, and *Achilles* commanded by Commodore Henry Harwood. The *Admiral Graf Spee* entered the battle and put the *Exeter* out of commission with its best weapons, but it also sustained damage and had to seek refuge in the Uruguayan harbor of Montevideo (therefore, not in Argentina).

Uruguay, concerned about maintaining neutrality, agreed to allow the ship to spend only three days in its harbor. On December 17, the *Graf Spee* set sail again and sank: Captain Hans Langsdorff had preferred to scuttle the ship instead of fighting a losing battle. In the meantime, Harwood's fourth ship, the *Cumberland*, had arrived to help the others that were awaiting the German ship just outside the harbor. Langsdorff killed himself two days later, to maintain his soldier's honor. Part of the German crew was imprisoned in Uruguay and a larger part was held in Argentina. Many of the sailors never returned to their homeland, and integrated into the existing Colonia Belgrano, a city in the province of Córdoba that was a typical center of German immigrants (ethnically similar to the Genovese settlement of Boca in Buenos Aires). The German ship bore the name of the admiral who had perished in the World War I in Argentinean territorial waters. The daughter of the late von Spee had christened it in 1934.

Therefore, Cristiani had confused an officer from WWI with a ship that had been named after him from WWII. And he imagined a relation between the expulsion from the harbor, which was fatal for the ship, and the desire for revenge against the country responsible for the expulsion.

That covers the war aspects, but this story would not be complete without a final note about its main character diplomat. The Count of Luxburg was christened Karl Ludwig, born in Würzburg on May 10, 1872. He had made his mark as a brilliant career diplomat in London, Rome, Cairo, St. Petersburg, and Peking. In 1912, he was Germany's Consul General to the English Indies and Ceylon. He came to Buenos Aires to manage business affairs in 1914, under the presidency of Victorino de la Plaza, and then the awkward naval incident unleashed pandemonium around him.

However, the most curious fact about the whole incident is that the Count of Luxburg returned to Argentina. Presumably uneasy around Hitler and his group, who rose to power in 1933, the Bavarese nobleman came back to Buenos Aires in 1933. He translated his given name to become Carlos Ludovico, worked in private business, and died as a serene *porteño* citizen on April 3, 1956 at the age of almost 84.

Appendix 4: Andrés Ducaud—Following Cristiani's Lead

THE ADVENTURES OF THE beginnings of Argentinean animation also involve Andrés Ducaud, the scenographer of *El Apóstol*. There is even less information about him than there is about Cristiani's work. Ducaud (who died in 1943) directed two animated films, probably feature length works, right after *El Apóstol* came out. In an attempt to avoid taking any particular stance on his work, it was decided to publish the translations of two more informed pieces that emerged during the research for this book. The first is by Jorge Miguel Couselo, titled "Aquellos primeros dibujos animados de largo metraje" (Those Early Animated Feature Films), in *Todo es historia*, cit.; the other is by Domingo di Núbila, *Historia del cine argentino*, cit., pp. 26–27.

Couselo wrote:

> Architect Ducaud was the main creative force behind *Abajo la careta* or *La república de Jauja* (Lower the Mask, or The Land-of-plenty Republic). It was a feature film made with

animated drawings, started immediately [after *El Apóstol*], and finished quickly enough to be projected on March 18, 1918 at the Grand Splendid, the Esmeralda, the Callao and the Petit Palace. [...] It was acclaimed as a production of Graphic Film, by Ducaud & Co. Incredibly, Andrés Ducaud continued to be an employee of Federico Valle, and this leads us to the conclusion that the film was probably sponsored by Valle, or that Valle, who was know for his generosity [*sic*], offered Ducaud the opportunity to make the movie that he wanted to make. Who were Ducaud's collaborators? We do not know.

"Intellectual minds collaborated to make this film, along with the best artists from the nation's capital," reported the very brief announcements. News broadcasts also failed to provide names, and the reproductions of the drawings that have survived to the present day bear only Ducaud's faded signature. The whole story is a mystery. However, the contents of that film are not a mystery.

The film may not have been directly Yrigoyenist or radical, but it aims its barbs at the regime in power before 1916. Also, there is no doubt about the fact that *La república de Jauja*, with 62,000 drawings and a duration that probably was similar to *El Apóstol*, followed its structure, taste in caricatures and meticulousness of political personalities and celebrities from A to Z. (We have heard there were 48 different characters!) The only difference was that the characters of the previous film were mainly radicals, but this time they belonged to the old oligarchy. However, ex-president Victorino de la Plaza appeared in the film but was not a protagonist—nobody was—as if they were not important. The subject, written by an unknown author, abandoned the previous allegory and went straight to the anecdotes, to show in less loaded images "the patterns of the top political factions" and "the intrigues of the bottom political factions" (according to the magazine *La Película*).

Along with well known faces, the film showed easily identified buildings, bustling city streets, and panoramic views of Buenos Aires. The film as a whole turns out to be less agile and tolerable than *El Apóstol*, if we consider another opinion from *La Película*: "[The movie] has the shortcoming of being vast, ornate, full of characters in action; the makers tried to encompass too wide a view, and this ideal extension bores the spectator […] There is no imagination that is capable of mentally absorbing such a vast theme as that which is proposed here." […] Ducaud continued to work with Valle, and right after this effort, *Abajo la careta*, they produced another feature film, *La Carmen criolla* or *Una noche de gala en el Colón* [Carmen Creole, or A Gala Evening at the Colón Theater'], which was satirical take on the elegant nightlife. Three dimensional puppets were used in this film instead of animated drawings."

di Núbila wrote:

When the financial returns were known [for *El Apóstol*], Valle and his men had already embarked on a new invention: a feature film made with puppets, in the same style of *anti-yrigoyenista* humor and satire as *El Apóstol*. The film was titled *Una noche de gala en el Colón*, and was also known as *Carmen Criolla*, because the story took place at the Colón theater during a gala presentation of Bizet's famous opera. It was divided into two parts. The first was done with animated puppets, and started in the atrium, with the arrival of illustrious personalities and the formation of small groups. The people continued to enter the auditorium and this part ends when everyone is seated. The second part was done with animated drawings, and showed the opera with Yrigoyen in the role of Carmen and his ministers and friends in the roles of Don José, Escamillo, Micaela, el Remendado, and the other characters. Cats make up the orchestra. The caricatures were created once again by "El Mono" Taborda, who drew them with greater realism, because an exaggeration would have been suitable for the drawn parts but not for the puppets. In addition to the well known Yrigoyen supporters, other important figures from that era were also included, such as Benito Villanueva, Julito Roca, Saavedra Lamas, and Guerrico Williams, and also Payo Roqué and also Negro Raúl [who was the image of the *porteña* gilded youth and the king of the inner city]. The only movie made with puppets before that time in Argentina was from *Cinematografia Valle*: just a few meters of film made on originals by Horacio Butler. For *Una noche de gala en el Colón*, a sculptor made clay models based on Taborda's original drawings and after correcting them slightly, molds were prepared and the final puppets were made and painted. Multiple heads were made for the puppets portraying the main characters, with different expressions and lip positions so that they would appear to be engaged in conversation if they were photographed in a certain order. Lastly, Ducaud tried to reproduce the scenography of the Colón theater as faithfully as possible in a very detailed model, but, just as in *El Apóstol*, the project turned out imperfect but just as interesting. It did not win the public's approval, but it was a useful experience for all those involved.

Decades later, Quirino Cristiani recalled the film *Una noche de gala en el Colón* as a feature film "made only with animated puppets." He also remembered that it was not successful "because the movement of the characters was imperfect, because it was not funny, and because the subject was not very interesting."

REFERENCES

Couselo, J. M. (1971). Aquellos primeros dibujos animados de largo metraje. *Todo es historia*, 47, Buenos Aires, March.

Cristiani, Q. (1917). *El Apóstol.*

di Núbila, D. (1960). *Historia del cine argentino.*

Ducaud, A. *La Carmen criolla.*

Ducaud, A. *Una noche de gala en el Colón.*

Index

Note: Page numbers followed by f refer to figures.